SEEING ALL THINGS WHOLE

"*Seeing All Things Whole* is a classic offering of 'theology as biography.' This is far more than a biography of one of the most influential leaders in the Wesleyan world. It is a deeper journey into a biblical theology of leadership which will inspire a whole new generation of leaders to serve Christ with dedication, clarity, and holiness."

—TIMOTHY C. TENNENT,
president, Asbury Theological Seminary

"This personal story reinforces the reality that theology is simply the story of God with us. David McKenna synthesizes experiences, people, and divine moments on his journey with God, modeling how to discover our place in that story of becoming whole. The journey is relational, descriptive, and summative. Through the vast experiences of his life, we are afforded gentle insight into the interweaving of personal surrender and the holiness of God that leads ultimately to wholeness."

—KEVIN MANNOIA,
founder, International Council for Higher Education

"David McKenna's latest book helps us capture the grand adventure of living our life as a response to the presence and love of God. In his 95th year, Dave continues to pursue God in ways unparalleled and unsurpassed. Always grateful for God's grace, Dave teaches us how to live a life of faithfulness not in spite of, but because of all that life brings."

—GAYLE D. BEEBE,
president, Westmont College

"In *Seeing All Things Whole*, David McKenna invites readers to journey through a life lived for Christ and the transformative power of faithful leadership. Together, David and his wife Jan model a faithfulness to God's call, even in the face of adversity, leaving an indelible mark on the campuses they led. The fruits of their labors are evident today at Seattle Pacific University and a testament to their legacy of leadership. McKenna's story is a guide for those who aspire to lead with authenticity, courage, and an unwavering trust in God's plan."

—DEANA PORTERFIELD,
president, Seattle Pacific University

"The Godfather of Christian Higher Education again reminds us all of the importance of a central unifying mission or life pursuit. In David McKenna's reflective memoir, his singular reason for Christian service stands clearly for all who read: to honor our Lord and Savior wholly, with heart, soul, and mind. McKenna's 'Passion for One, Compassion for All' sounds a clarion call for the next generation of Christian leaders to hold unwaveringly to our commitment to Christ and to express that commitment through tangible acts of love and service to others, regardless of the consequences."

—BRENT ELLIS,
president, Spring Arbor University

"David McKenna opens the book of his life in the pages of *Seeing All Things Whole*. With higher education as the backdrop, he shares his wisdom from the lessons learned in life spent searching for calling, purpose, and holiness. In his stories, we see the times when the impossible becomes possible and how faith is strengthened by what cannot be seen or fully understood. May all who read this learn to recognize the *high tides of life* and embrace them."

—TAMI HEIM,
president and CEO, Christian Leadership Alliance

Seeing All Things Whole

My Calling to Fulfill

DAVID L. McKENNA

RESOURCE *Publications* · Eugene, Oregon

SEEING ALL THINGS WHOLE
My Calling to Fulfill

Resource Publications
An Imprint of Wipf and Stock Publishers
199 W. 8th Ave., Suite 3
Eugene, OR 97401

www.wipfandstock.com

PAPERBACK ISBN: 979-8-3852-2275-9
HARDCOVER ISBN: 979-8-3852-2276-6
EBOOK ISBN: 979-8-3852-2277-3
VERSION NUMBER 07/17/24

Dedicated to:
Jan
My First Lady
for
75 years

To serve the present age,
My calling to fulfill;
O, may it all my pow'rs engage
To do my Master's will.

CHARLES WESLEY

Contents

Acknowledgments

An author's richest resource is faithful friends who are also loving critics. Because autobiographical writing is so delicately balanced on the scales of self-revelation, I have not hesitated to ask my friends and colleagues to read this text with these questions in mind: Does the story flow? Does it probe the depths of my mind and heart? Is the Holy Spirit the author behind the author? Is the outcome redemptive? Is God glorified?

I am indebted to all those who read the text, answered the questions, and endorsed the book. They include Gayle Beebe, president of Westmont College, Brent Ellis, president of Spring Arbor University, Deana Porterfield, president of Seattle Pacific University, Timothy Tennent, president of Asbury Theological Seminary, Tami Heim, President and CEO, Christian Leadership Alliance, and Kevin Mannoia, Founder, International Council for Higher Education.

Our daughter, Debra, and our sons, Douglas and Rob, were my in-family readers whose insights went right to the heart of the story, sometimes applauding, sometimes correcting, but always encouraging me to keep writing. Joining them with comments and suggestions were close friends, David Goodnight, Shirley Ort, Greg Asimakoupoulus, and Kimberly Rupert. As always, I counted on Sheila Lovell, my Executive Assistant at Asbury Theological Seminary, to do the final review and copyediting before publication. Thanks to all who encouraged me to continue writing into my middle 90s with no reduction in expectations for quality and inspiration.

David L. McKenna

Introduction

The Odyssey Continues From Grace to Grace

READERS OF MY BOOK *The Triumphs of His Grace: A Spiritual Odyssey* rightfully ask, *"How do you account for the change from a 17-year-old boy escaping the confines of a radical Holiness tabernacle to the presidency of three Christian institutions of higher learning and a leadership role in the world Wesleyan movement?"*

The gap is so great that my story teeters on the edge of disbelief. True to form, it is an odyssey or a pilgrimage more than a journey and a trek more than a trip. It would be false to assume some magic jump from being a boy in a holiness tabernacle to a college, university and seminary president. The story in between those years may not be quite as dramatic as my Tabernacle years, but the evidence of the threads of grace being woven into the whole cloth of God's perfect will is just as clear and inspiring. Thus, the odyssey continues under the title *Seeing All Things Whole: My Calling to Fulfill.* It begins from the time that I walked away from the Tabernacle as a high school senior to the present time when I am 95 years old and president emeritus of three institutions of Christian higher education. Looking back on the years between the day I left the Tabernacle and to this day of reflection in retirement, I see my continuing odyssey progressing through these stages:

1. The Call Received – remembering the key intersections in my spiritual odyssey where I learned the meaning of holiness and wholeness;

2. The Call Answered – recapturing what I learned as a president of three institutions of Christian higher education about holiness and wholeness;

3. The Call Extended – reminiscing through the professional relationships in the larger Wesleyan and Evangelical world in which I applied my understanding of holiness and wholeness.

What is the perspective from which I invite you to read? The answer is in the words that David Hubbard, President of Fuller Theological Seminary, chose when he introduced me at a national theological conference,

"Our speaker today is David McKenna, The Great Synthesizer."

At first, I felt as if David had couched a sarcastic cut in a humorous compliment. In the company of theologians who relish debate on the number of angels who can dance on the head of a pin, was I seen as a seminary president who had no claim to scholarship except putting together borrowed thoughts? The question passed quickly because I knew that David, a close friend, would never insult me. Instead, he held up a mirror in which I could see myself as others see me,--a Christian with a Wesleyan perspective who has spent a lifetime in the search and discovery mission for holiness and wholeness, but both personally and professionally.

THE UNFINISHED QUEST

I closed *The Triumphs of His Grace: A Spiritual Odyssey* with ominous words to sum up my Tabernacle days: "I left and never looked back." Later, after reflecting on the experience, I changed my conclusion to read, "I left with my freedom as a flame and holiness as my thirst." Try as I might, I could not escape the awakening in which the Spirit of God led me on a quest for truth as a student at Spring Arbor Junior College (now University), a pastor at Vicksburg, Michigan, a graduate student at Asbury Theological Seminary, and a faculty member at The Ohio State University and the University of Michigan. Not only did I find the touchstone for my faith during this quest, but I also discovered the tenets of truth for the grounding of my faith. From this position of strength, I began the journey through my professional career as president of Spring Arbor University, Seattle Pacific University, and Asbury Theological Seminary. In concert with these callings, I also need to tell the story of my relationships with the Free Methodist Church, The World Methodist Council, and the National Association of Evangelicals. Whether in professional career or in these professional relationships, I see my mission as embracing and extending John Wesley's unforgettable words, *"The gospel of Christ knows no religion but social; no holiness but social holiness."*[1] It is a love story, but not without recognition of a lifetime of struggles against the sins of self-interest. Nor is it without criticism and a plea for renewal of theological, ecclesiastical, and societal distinctives in the schools I love and the relationships I cherish. As we know from scripture, whenever and wherever the Spirit of God touches down in physical creation or human nature, brokenness is transformed into a wholeness that is far greater than the sum of its parts and a beauty that reflects God's grand design. From this perspective I dare to look toward a future with both its toxic threats and its transformative potential. I do not claim to be "The Great Synthesizer," but I do claim that my thirst for the experience of holiness has led me to see the evidence of all things whole in every dimension of my life and work. Without equivocation, I can say that my deepest desire is to share in John Wesley's vision of wholeness:

> *I want the whole Christ as my savior, the whole Bible as my guide, the whole Church as my fellowship, and the whole world as my mission field.*

Thus, my spiritual odyssey continues. To begin, I trace salient moments of my life and career that confirm my God-given vision for, "Seeing All Things Whole." In each case, the subtitle, "My Calling to Fulfill" comes forward as a reminder that our calling is a lifelong quest toward completion, not completion in itself. As my final word, I write a Reprise under the title "God's Grand Design," inviting the reader to celebrate with me the joy of being a role

---

1. Wesley and Wesley, *Hymns and Sacred Poems,* 1739, Preface, p. viii.

player in the redemptive drama where the beauty of the whole is greater than the sum of its parts. Together, then, we can sense the lift of freedom that comes when we are maturing in holiness as our experience and wholeness as its evidence.

I

The Call Received

1

The Spring Arbor Bypass
A Beloved Mentor

PAUL HARVEY'S PATENTED ENDING, "Now for the rest of the story," always promised a good ending for a challenging story. After posing a problem, he then pulled a thread of hope through to an affirmative end. My book, *The Triumphs of His Grace: A Spiritual Odyssey*, follows the same path. In each chapter you can see and feel the onerous weight of religious strictures, fractured faith, and pessimistic attitudes that can lead to disillusionment with the established church, if not rejection of the faith itself. But every chapter also has a thread of grace that gives promise of a redemptive outcome. It is these threads of grace that I want to follow into a future where holiness is my experience and wholeness is my evidence. Re-echoing Harvey, I am bold to say, "Now for the rest of the story."

A DIVINE CONNECTION

Start with my birth as an unwanted child, add the miracle of prayer when death lurked, follow the path through a suffocating religious childhood, and come to a high school senior's search for a Christian college. Despite the opposition to higher education in the Evangelistic Mission Tabernacle where our family worshipped, my parents traveled with me from Ypsilanti, Michigan to Marion, Indiana with the view toward enrollment at Marion College, an educational institution of the Wesleyan Church. For some reason, nothing clicked on our visit, but on the way home on Saturday night we stopped at a grocery store in Coldwater, Michigan to buy a roast for our Sunday dinner. A card on the meat counter of Reppert's Grocery announced a revival meeting at the local Free Methodist Church with a picture of the evangelist, Rev. Harry Hosmer. Simultaneously, while we were reading the announcement, the front door opened, and Rev. Hosmer walked in. For a reason known only to God, my father went up to him and said, "I went to Ypsilanti High School with your sister." The providential connection was made and then pursued by my mother, who inserted, "We are looking for a Christian college for our son." A new voice entered the conversation when Rev. Hosmer's son, Harry Jr., following close behind his father and sporting a high school varsity jacket, piped up, "Have you tried Spring Arbor?"

The name brought up a blank. Neither my parents nor I had ever heard of Spring Arbor. Into the blank space, Harry Jr. gave one of the most effective PR pitches for Spring Arbor Junior College, a Free Methodist educational institution just outside Jackson, Michigan. He finished by suggesting that we take M-60 home through Spring Arbor and Jackson rather than following the straight route on US-12 from Coldwater to Ypsilanti, Michigan.

We opted for the Spring Arbor bypass. It was dark when we arrived at the campus, but a luminous moon highlighted the buildings, especially the half-completed men's residence hall. The moonlight image is forever fixed in my mind. Peacefulness of spirit matched the soft tones of the evening sky. I said to my parents, "This is it." Two days later, I enrolled as a student on a scholarship and work study program to meet my tuition.

I WAS HOME!

THE THREAD OF DESTINY

At Spring Arbor Junior College, I met the man whom I consider the most significant model and mentor in my life. He is directly responsible for changing my view of Wesleyan holiness from fractured perfectionism to holistic beauty, Dr. James Gregory served as President of the school even though he lacked the image and flair of an administrative leader. With the reserve of his Canadian ancestry and the gentle presence of the Holy Spirit, he guided Spring Arbor by example more than tactics and by teaching more than pronouncements.

I met President Gregory as professor for my first class in Christian Theology. Without a doubt, I count him as the best teacher I ever had. The memory of one class will last forever. When the class progressed to the doctrine of entire sanctification, I brought all of my rebellion from the past with me. If holiness of heart still meant instant perfection or imperious purity, I wanted no part of it. Dr. Gregory, however, walked us through the passages of scripture that draw us toward our personal Pentecost as well as those that command us to be holy. In sum, he said that the doctrine of entire sanctification means, "*As believers surrender to God and die to self through full consecration, the Holy Spirit fills us with love and purifies us from sin.*"[1] Then, with the stroke of the master teacher, our president and professor said, "Let me show you what I mean." He reached to the shoulder of his blue-serge suit, pulled out a thread from the fabric, and stretched it out before us. I can still hear the clipped, but soft, sound of his Canadian accent as he said,

> "As you can see, the thread I hold has the texture and tone of the whole cloth. Likewise, when we are sanctified, every thread of our being will carry the texture and tone of the Spirit of God and the life of Christ."

I count that moment as the acme of all my learning experience and, most important, my sanctifying moment. By pulling through the thread of grace that existed just below the surface in

---

1. 2019 *Free Methodist Church Book of Discipline*, 121.

Tabernacle terms, Dr. Gregory showed me how wholeness is the evidence of holiness, not just in our hearts, but in every facet of our believing, being and doing. With the simplest of illustrations, he made Wesleyan holiness my vision, my challenge and my discipline through all the years of my life. For good reason, I count Dr. James Gregory as the one who helped me see past the burden of holiness to the beauty of wholeness.

A CHASTENING TO REMEMBER

All of my experiences with President Gregory were not as positive. In my sophomore year at Spring Arbor, I was President of my class with a roommate who was captain of the basketball team. At Homecoming, we decided to rebel against the tradition of presenting our dormitory rooms to our parents as models of cleanliness and creativity. Our rebellion surfaced as a red carpet leading to a cardboard box that had a hole shaped like the opening in an outhouse and complete with a ripped Sears catalog on the side. Somehow, word about the fiasco leaked to President Gregory and he ordered our door closed as parents walked through the dorm. He also sent word for me to report to the President's office the first thing on Monday morning, I was petrified, especially when I entered his office and saw the face behind the desk. All gentleness had disappeared and without a greeting he only nodded me into the single seat that directly faced him. Then, with a sternness I had never known, he spoke,

> "David, there are certain proprieties in Western culture that we must honor, not just as Christians, but as decent human beings. There is nothing humorous about your outhouse scene, especially at Homecoming when parents and guests are visitors in the dorm. If something like this happens again, you will be expelled. For now, you are dismissed."

I had never taken such a beating, except when I disappointed my father by using his money and taking his car to the movies.

Although President Gregory spoke with cold anger, I could sense the deep hurt in him.

The lesson is unforgettable. President Gregory held me accountable for my actions, particularly my leadership. In sharpest contrast with the arrogance of autocracy that I had seen in the Tabernacle, I left his office with the vow to always be humble and accountable if God called me into leadership. Without a doubt, after my natural father denied the Christ, James Gregory took his place as my spiritual father. Whether in praise or punishment, the threads of grace were being woven into the call of God for both holiness and wholeness.

A LASTING LEGACY

Just five years after my learning experience in the President's office and the tutelage of the Holy Spirit, I returned to Spring Arbor as Dean of Men and Instructor in Religion. Dr. Gregory had gone on to serve the Free Methodist denomination as Editor of *Light and Life* magazine, official organ of the Church. His journalistic skills made his editorial column a "must" reading for me.

More years passed. I had been promoted to Dean of the College at Spring Arbor and achieved candidacy for the Ph.D at the University of Michigan. Then, the news came, Dr. Gregory had died and his funeral would be in Winona Lake, Indiana, denominational home for the Free Methodist Church. Of course, I attended the services and gave condolences to his widow, Freda. To my surprise, she asked if I could stop by their home after the service to pick up something that her husband had left for me. A life-changing moment awaited me. In his final will, Dr. Gregory left me a note expressing his confidence in me and my ministry along with three gifts. He bequeathed to me his doctoral cap and gown, a copy of Thomas A'Kempis' *Imitation of Christ* and C.S. Lewis' *Surprised by Joy*. What a legacy! Although the doctoral gown was too short for me, I wore it for commencements and formal addresses for many years. Then, when the time came to get a new gown for presidential functions, I bequeathed Dr. Gregory's gown to our oldest son, David Douglas McKenna when he earned his Ph.D in Differential Psychology at the University of Minnesota. Now, with its colors still intact and the velvet still smooth, the gown has been given to our grandson, Sean David Kinzer, who earned his Ph.D in Computer Science and Computer Engineering in 2024 from the University of California San Diego. Thus, the legacy lives on. I have no doubt Dr. Gregory saw in me what I did not see in myself. Future presidencies at Spring Arbor University, Seattle Pacific University, and Asbury Theological Seminary confirm his confidence.

As for the prized volumes of *Imitation of Christ* and *Surprised by Joy*, Thomas A'Kempis' Catholicism and C. S. Lewis' tankard of ale with an ever-present pipe would have cancelled them from the reading list at the Tabernacle. Dr. Gregory, however, must have seen them as vehicles for vision as I advanced through my academic career and tested the waters of the larger Christian world. *The Imitation of Christ* is unparalleled for genuine spirituality and *Surprised by Joy* sounds a grace note that makes our spirituality not just joyful, but jubilant. For good reason, they are both prominently displayed in my study, and I am quick to tell the story when anyone asks why. With just two books, my mentor foresaw in me the possibilities of an ecumenical spirit and an evangelical thrust that I embrace with joy. To think it all began in a theology class when President James Gregory showed me the beauty of Biblical holiness and then proceeded to show me how to live it out in the remainder of my life. His influence set me on a search and discovery mission in The Word of God for the threads of grace out of which God was weaving the whole cloth of His will for my life. Even more important, I ask, "*What is the message of hope that we offer to a broken world and a fractured generation?*" Our answer must be grounded in the Word of God. Therefore, as the next step in my spiritual odyssey, I invite my readers to join me for the short stay at our first and only parish in the village of Vicksburg, Michigan. I count the short time there as another step toward fulfillment in the whole will of God.

2

The Vicksburg Stopover
A Village Parish

AFTER GRADUATION FROM SPRING Arbor Junior College, I looked forward to finishing my undergraduate work at Greenville College, a senior college of The Free Methodist Church. The decision depended upon getting a scholarship along with a campus job in order to pay my way. As part of their denominational relationship with Spring Arbor, Greenville provided full scholarship aid to the valedictorian and salutatorian of the graduating class. When I was named salutatorian of the 1949 graduating class my hopes were buoyed and I began to make plans to attend Greenville.

Commencement smashed my dream. Even though I was salutatorian the Board of Trustees made the decision to jump from second to twelfth place in the ranking of scholarly achievement and award the grant to James Hudson Taylor II, grandson of one of the greatest of China missionaries, Hudson Taylor. James and his Free Methodist missionary family had been interred in Chinese prison camps during World War II and released with the surrender of Japan. Certainly, he deserved the scholarship. Add the fact that James was my best friend at Spring Arbor. We played vicious tennis together and spent hours debating theology. After our freshman year, we hitchhiked cross-country in order to be youth evange-lists in Free Methodist camp meetings on the East coast. James was the celebrity who had a dramatic story of being imprisoned in China while I served as backup praying for youthful penitents at the altar of prayer. After our first camp meeting in New Jersey we were scheduled to travel to Massachusetts as the next stop. With a bit of chagrin, I confess that I had fallen madly in love with Janet, pastor's daughter of the Spring Arbor Church. So, when the New Jersey camp meeting closed I took the first bus home. Thus ended my non-illustrious ministry as a youth evangelist.

James had to go it alone at the Massachusetts camp-meeting. His faithfulness matched his heart-rending story of separation from his parent and imprisonment in a Japanese concentration camp. James Hudson Taylor deserved the Greenville scholarship, but it left me without the funds to pay the tuition and costs of my junior and senior years of college.

As a bit of ironic humor in the story, after graduation from Spring Arbor I received a phone call from Dr. Henry J. Long, Presi-dent of Greenville College. To compensate for my loss of the schol-arship he offered me a service grant and a work study program to meet my college costs. For the service grant he said, "David. Our college quartet needs your voice. I will have the other three mem-bers meet you at the train station." Then, knowing that the service scholarship for traveling with the college quartet would not meet my costs, President Long asked if I had a union card as a mason or carpenter for work constructing the new library. Of course, I had no such skill or credential. My hope for attending Greenville was dashed again.

Both my plans and my dreams for completing my under-graduate education at a Christian college were never realized. Instead, I opted to return home to Ypsilanti, Michigan and attend Eastern Michigan University. When I returned to reconnect with my high school classmates, I realized how far apart we had grown. Their idea of success was to pledge at the best-known fraternity or sorority and their idea of happiness was a party with a full cask of beer. Even though I was elected as a pledge to both the music and football fraternities, I had no interest in membership.

Meanwhile, my love for Jan grew deeper and more serious. At Christmas, 1949, I asked her to marry me. In keeping with the Free Methodist ethos at that time, I gave her a hope chest rather an engagement ring. When we were married (without wedding rings) on June 9, 1950 in the Spring Arbor Free Methodist Church the college quartet sang the wedding march acapella because instrumental music was not allowed. What a far cry from the piano, horns, drums and guitars of the Evangelistic Mission Tabernacle!

Even though Eastern Michigan is a public university without a religion department I continued to hold my calling as a minister of the Gospel that I had received during my Tabernacle years. The Rev. E.A. Cutler, Superintendent of the Southern Michigan Conference of the Free Methodist Church knew of my calling and encouraged me to pursue ministerial credentials. With his blessing, I applied for membership in the Conference and soon learned that Rev. Cutler had a plan to appoint me to the parish at Vicksburg, Michigan so that I could complete my bachelor's degree at Western Michigan University in nearby Kalamazoo. When Rev. Cutler announced his plans in a general session of the Conference, he blew all of the fuses of bias among a cadre of members. Leading the way was a delegate from Detroit who had intimate knowledge about The Evangelistic Mission Tabernacle and its churches in Pontiac, Adrian, and Garden City as well as Ypsilanti. With a voice rising from loud to angry, he degraded my past and made a motion to deny me membership in the Conference. After his diatribe was finished and he sat down, Rev. Cutler stepped the mike with his authority as Conference Superintendent and gave his response. "I don't care what you do with your vote, I know this man and I am giving him a church today."

Hush fell over the assembly as the delegates contemplated their decision. Finally, from one corner of the room a single clap of the hands was heard followed by the sweeping sound of applause from the audience as well as the delegates. Thus, in dramatic fashion, I was inducted into Free Methodism as a ministerial candidate along with appointment as the pastor of the Church in Vicksburg, Michigan, a small parish of 35 members known as the last stop for retiring preachers or, in our case, a 21-year-old kid finishing his college degree.

We always get a laugh to remember that Jan was just 19 years old when she took on the title of "Sister McKenna" among women members whose ages ranged up into the 80's and whose hair had never been styled except by bobby pins. One day Jan made the mistake of going to the beauty shop for a cut and curl. When she appeared for the morning service the next Sunday, she faced the scrutiny of her sisters and at the next Tuesday morning prayer meeting, they "waited on her" for her sin. Jan never told me about the prayer meeting because she knew that their verbal condemnation would be nothing compared to my wrath if I found out.

Despite such little snags, our year at Vicksburg proved to be a Godsend for us. Each morning, I drove to Kalamazoo taking a full load as a senior majoring in history at Western Michigan University. Returning home after classes, I took on the pastoral duties of calling on members, preparing sermons, and doing the duties of a janitor in the grubby little church. Lasting memories of the year include the conversion of Dick and Fran, our neighbors who befriended us, remodeling of the interior of Church to make it a welcome place, mentoring a delightful core of teenagers in the youth group, and welcoming Bishop Charles Fairbairn for rededication of the remodeled sanctuary.

During this time, Jan became pregnant so that we had to revise our plan following the will of God to enroll at Asbury Theological Seminary the following fall. Once again Jan's commitment to the call of God stands tall. She said that I should go alone to Asbury until the baby was born. She was a pastor's daughter who knew the price of the itinerant ministry. Without hesitation, she moved in with her parents in the parsonage of The Free Methodist Church in Ann Arbor, Michigan and worked as a nurse's aide the University of Michigan Hospital until late in her term. My debt to her can never be paid.

3

The Wilmore Junction
A Timeless Call

IN THE EARLY FALL of 1950, I drove alone from Ann Arbor, Michigan to Wilmore, Kentucky to enroll at Asbury Theological Seminary. While waiting for our baby to come, I resided in the men's residence facility on the top floor of Morrison Hall, the administration building. My roommate was a student from China who claimed to be an atheist but used enrollment in the Seminary as a way to enter the United States. I saw little of my roommate except when he came in late at night and lay in bed crunching the Chinese delicacy of crickets.

On November 7, 1950, I received the call from my father. He announced that Jan's labor pains were only a few minutes apart and they were heading for the University of Michigan hospital for the delivery. At break-neck speed I drove the 330 miles from Wilmore to Ann Arbor along two and four lane roads in just 6 1/2 hours. When I arrived at the hospital, I rushed to the desk and asked to see my wife. The receptionist checked the patient's list and reported that no Janet McKenna was registered. I was ready to say, "She has to be" when the door opened and Jan walked in with our parents close behind. Ten hours later our son, David Douglas, was born. After a couple days at home, I had to drive back to Wilmore to finish the fall semester and prepare the apartment for the arrival of Jan and Douglas shortly after the New Year's break.

THE CALL OF INDIA

As always, I was a student in a hurry. To save money and support my family, I crammed three years of seminary into two including summers at the Institution for Pastoral Care at the University of Michigan. In my senior year at Asbury Theological Seminary, I was on a fast track toward a Ph.D in Pastoral Psychology. Two offers were in my hands, one on the East coast and one on the West coast. In the East I had been accepted for the Ph.D at Boston University and, to support my young family, a pastorate awaited us at the Free Methodist Church in Situate, Massachusetts. On the other coast, I had acceptance for the Ph.D in Pastoral Psychology at the University of Southern California and a contract in hand to teach religion and psychology at Los Angeles Pacific College, a Free Methodist institution. As I weighed the merits of both offers, I put a premium on the needs of Janet, my wife, and Douglas, our 7-month-old son. Consequently, the desire to teach at LAPC was balanced by the presence of a parsonage in Massachusetts. In both cases, I also struggled with a move to either the East or West coast that would take us away from family and friends in Michigan, especially Jan's aging parents who lived in Spring Arbor.

In the midst of my deliberations, I attended a chapel service where Dr. J.T. Seamands, an esteemed missionary from India, was featured as the morning speaker. After Dr. Seamands described the dire needs of Indian people for the Gospel and cited the joy of his own work, he asked his seminary audience the question, "Is God calling you to India?" The question immediately snagged my spirit and I heard the unmistakable voice of God calling me to India. Confusion mixed with rebellion swept over me and I did not join the students at the altar who were responding to Dr. Seamands' invitation. Instead, I skipped my next class and went straight home to our little apartment to duel with the Spirit of God while kneeling bedside. I asked God, "How could I have two acceptances for Ph.D studies in my hand along with assurance of support for my young family and yet receive the conflicting call to India?" The struggle lasted for more than an hour as I continued to question the wisdom of God, making my case for a contradiction between His guidance in the past and His promise for the future. Finally, after a rebellious hour or more passed, I realized that the Spirit of God was not letting up. The call to go India was the clearest call that I had ever received. So, putting self-interest to death, I told the Lord, "I will go to India even if I never receive a Ph.D." With that commitment, the tension went away and I was at peace. To seal my vow, I also prayed, "Lord, if you open the doors for India, I will be on the first plane out." Without the slightest doubt, this commitment to do the whole will of God is an ever-present vow that continues until this every moment. It adds another thread of grace to the whole cloth of God's perfect will for my life. Most of all, it is experiential confirmation of my sanctifying moment when I invited the Holy Spirit to have full sway in every aspect of my life, present as well as future.

Meanwhile, I was still in the throes of making a decision between offers from the East coast and West coast. As I recall, I definitely favored going to southern California because of the opportunity to teach at Los Angeles Pacific College. The scale was almost tipped when I had a surprise call from Dr. Charlie Moon, President of Spring Arbor Junior College. With the precision for which he was known, Dr. Moon wasted no time to tell me that my alma mater was calling me back to take the position as Dean of Men (living in the family apartment of Ormston Hall, the site of my first vision of Spring Arbor) and Instructor in Psychology and Sociology. This position would allow me to complete my Ph.D at the University of Michigan in the field of Higher Education Administration. Three attractive offers now compounded my dilemma. I am not sure how carefully I put all of them on the table and weighed them equally. But, as expected by now, we opted for the position at Spring Arbor as an answer to our prayers with all of the advantages of going home, being near our parents, serving the school we loved, and attending the university of our dreams. We did not know whether this decision meant another Spring Arbor bypass on the way to India, but we never took back our commitment, "If God opens the door with the call to India, we will be on the first plane out."

Our tenure at Spring Arbor Junior College began as Dean of Men and Instructor in Psychology and Sociology. After two years in those positions, Dr. Moon invited me to be Dean of the Junior College with the primary responsibility of achieving state and regional accreditation for the school. The challenge fit perfectly with my preparation. After doing a self-study and presenting an oral presentation in support of our case, we were recognized in 1956 by the Michigan Commission of College and University Accreditation as a fully accredited two-year college. Our next goal was to achieve regional accreditation with the North Central Accrediting Commission. After another self-study and educational improvement according to North Central standards, we received approval in 1958. Perhaps in recognition of our achievement I was appointed Chair of the Michigan Commission on College and University and leading accreditation visits to other independent schools in the State.

In addition to my responsibilities at Spring Arbor, I enrolled for a full load of graduate study at the University of Michigan. Each Monday, Wednesday and Friday I left Spring Arbor early in the morning to drive 60 miles to Ann Arbor and catch my first of two classes. Shortly before noon, then, I drove back to Spring Arbor just in time to teach Introduction to Psychology followed by Introduction to Sociology. Later, I had to add Saturday for one semester in order to finish my course work for the Ph.D. As time went on, I realized that I had become the favorite student of Dr. Algo Henderson, Director of the Center for the Study of Higher Education. The proof came when he and his wife invited Jan and me to join them for dinner at the home of Harlan Hatcher, President of the University of Michigan. It is a moment to remember. President and Mrs. Hatcher were the most sophisticated, but gracious, couple we had ever met. The conversation centered around

Dr. Henderson's review of his program using me as his example. A high table dinner was then served by white-jacketed stewards. Jan and I excused ourselves from the drinks before, during and after dinner, but without feeling embarrassed. Later, I realized what Dr. Henderson was trying to do. He wanted to introduce me as his prize student and prepare the way for me as his future replacement.

Meanwhile, the next logical step for Spring Arbor was advancement to a four-year Christian liberal arts college. Because the new president, Roderick Smith, was a young man with good credentials for leadership in public schools, I felt as if my future was limited as vice-president with responsibility for another round of work in a self-study for regional accreditation. Privately, I began to search for a new challenge in executive leadership, preferably but not exclusively, in Christian higher education.

4

The Columbus Connection
The Whole Cloth

My wish for a new challenge in higher education came in the spring of 1960. Dr. Algo Henderson recommended me for a faculty position at The Ohio State University with the goal of founding a Center for the Study of Higher Education similar to the one at the University of Michigan. I am not sure that I can claim full attention to the will of God for the decision that followed, but I do thank Him for His patience. After an interview with Ohio State deans and directors, I received the invitation to the position. We again went into decision-making mode. In one sense we had accomplished our goals at Spring Arbor. The Ohio State invitation would launch me into a leadership role in the rapidly developing field of Higher Education as an independent discipline. Countering the attraction of the offer, I again had to make decisions for our family. We had Douglas, 9, and Debra, 4, along with the expectation for our third child in November. Because I would be engaged in the crucial months of a new career, Jan would have to carry the weight of homemaking with two young children and a new baby. Reflecting back upon those crucial hours and days, I can only again give thanks for Jan's early experience as the daughter of an in itinerant Free Methodist pastor. Add her sacrificial love and her understanding of my ambition, and we made the decision to move so that I could test the waters of public higher education.

Our memories of our year at Ohio State are all good, with one exception. We lived in an up-and-down apartment in Upper Arlington among other young couples and families. Our arrival in the company of Jan's elderly parents came on the eve of the 4th of July. When night fell, the celebrating began. Up and down the street fireworks went off and the sounds of drunken parties came through open doors. I can still see the look in the eyes of Janet's mother. As a Free Methodist pastor's wife from the quiet village of Spring Arbor, she reflected the question, "What have you done to my daughter?"

As a counterforce to this new encounter with a secular society, the Columbus Free Methodist Church, its pastor and people, warmly welcomed us into their community of faith. Credit also belongs to the faculty of the School of Education. Even though I was the most visible theist in their ranks, they welcomed me as a colleague and friend. In my interview with the faculty where my credentials in Christian higher education were reviewed, one professor took the floor and growled, "What is a theist doing in a place like this?" He was shouted down by multiple voices shouting, "Why not? What's wrong about being a theist?" In short order I was approved by a faculty that had the reputation of being the most ardent disciples of John Dewey and his antagonism to Christianity.

As soon as I arrived at Ohio State, Christian students quickly found me. Within a month of arrival, I was a faculty advisor for InterVarsity Christian Fellowship on the campus. I do recall one little glitch among the good news. When I agreed to teach a Sunday School class at the Free Methodist Church, the Associate Dean of the School of Law heard about it and came to the class each Sunday (he never stayed for the worship service) to contest the faith with me. A self-acclaimed agnostic, he challenged every point I made, much to the delight of the class members. To say the least, I learned how to contend for the faith once delivered in a setting a bit like Paul's debates with the Greeks at the Acropolis.

The highlight of my Ohio State time was leadership for President Novice Fawcett on the study of the trimester system as an alternative to the quarter system on the academic calendar. Interviews with the president and his staff along with every vice-president and dean in the university gave me an experience in the administration of higher education that was worth years of service in those positions. After only twelve months at Ohio State, my dream for a Center for the Study of Higher Education became smashed like the reflection of a rainbow in an oil spill. While preparing to present my model for the Center, I received a call from the Dean of the College of Education. Memory still sees the rings of smoke rising from his pipe as he spoke slowly and deliberately, "David, the Ohio State legislature has cut the budget and along with all new programs for the University. You will have to be ready to make a long-term investment in order to see a Center for the Study of Higher Education come to life." While still working through my disappointment, I received the phone call from Dr. Algo Henderson inviting me to be the Assistant Director of the Center for the Study of Higher Education at the University of Michigan. Some might call it luck, but I call it providence. Perhaps my sojourn at Ohio State was a side-road in my career, but it was invaluable preparation for the presidency.

REFLECTION ON THE WHOLE CLOTH

With the image of The Whole Cloth always before us, the stage was now set for the rest of the story. Beginning with chronicles on the three institutions of Christian higher education where I served as president and adding the three areas of Christian witness to which I was called, you will understand why I have chosen *Seeing All Things Whole: My Calling to Fulfill* as the title for this book. In a very real sense, it is the sequel to my earlier book, *The Triumphs of His Grace: A Spiritual Odyssey.* The titles are different, but the story is the same. Through threads of grace and truth, the experiences of my life are being woven into the whole cloth of God's perfect will. Even at the age of 95, the story is not over. Day by day,

I still see threads of grace that are being woven into the story of our retirement years. Best of all, I do not fix my gaze on the knots that make up the underside of my life's tapestry, but on the beauty of the design on the topside. With all joy, I give thanks to God for letting me get a glimpse of the whole cloth.

ON WITH THE ODYSSEY

With the affirmations of the Holy Spirit clearly in mind, return with me to the spiritual odyssey begun in *The Triumphs of His Grace*. My quest for holiness and wholeness continued into my education as a college student earning a bachelor's degree in history and as a graduate student completing advanced degrees in theology, psychology and higher education administration. My call to ministry was still crystal clear, but now I saw the pastoral implications for the presidency in Christian higher education. The college campus became my parish, and the faculty and students became my congregation. In each of the positions and places where I served in my professional career of 41 years, I saw my calling confirmed and my commitment to personal and social holiness reinforced time and time again. What started out as the sanctifying moment that I experienced at Spring Arbor Junior College became my heartbeat for a "World Parish" in the academic realm. I can only marvel and give thanks for the diverse threads of grace that were woven together into the fabric of a life and a career given to God and crowned by the beauty of His holiness.

II

The Call Answered

5

Spring Arbor University
The Big Idea

I CAME TO THE college presidency out of a conflicted decision. In 1961, after a year as a Professor at The Ohio State University, I signed a contract with the Center for the Study of Higher Education at the University of Michigan. We were ready to make the move when Hugh A. White, Chair of the Board at Spring Arbor Junior College, called and invited us to the presidency of our alma mater. His call caused a soul-wrenching conflict within me. On one hand, I had signed a contract to teach at Michigan and serve as Assistant Director of the Center for the Study of Higher Education, the acknowledged leader in the nation for producing presidents of universities and colleges. On the other hand, I sensed the deep love that I had for Spring Arbor Junior College, the place I revered because it was there that I saw the beauty of holiness in the whole cloth of God's will. I also felt a debt of love for Spring Arbor because it was there that I met Janet, my wife.

The conflict took us to fasting and prayer. Would we follow our hearts in response to the call of God or would we honor the contract that held such promise for identity as a leader in American higher education? The answer came in an unexpected way.

When Jan and I searched for a home in Ann Arbor, home of the University of Michigan, we came up empty. Then, the person who bought our home in Spring Arbor when we made the move to Ohio State suddenly reneged on his contract and left us with a vacant house. Our dilemma deepened. We had little leverage for the purchase of a home in Ann Arbor and the real estate market in Spring Arbor was flat. So, we decided to put the decision to the acid test. I would go to Dr. Algo Henderson, Director of the Center for the Study of Higher Education and lay out my dilemma. If he held us to the contract, we would go to Michigan. If he freed us from the contract, we would go to Spring Arbor.

AN AGNOSTIC'S SACRIFICE

The day of decision will never be forgotten. Janet, with our children, Douglas, 9, Debra, 4, and Suzanne, five months, along with her parents waited on the lawn of Bill Knapp's restaurant on the outskirts of Ann Arbor while I met with Dr. Henderson in his office at the University. Fear and trepidation were my emotions as I spun out my dilemma and concluded by saying that my first obligation was to honor the University of Michigan contract. I can still see Dr. Henderson spinning a paper clip as he responded so thoughtfully to me. "David," he said, "I sense your love for Spring Arbor. It will be our loss, but if you are compelled to follow your love, we will be proud to have you in the presidency. After all, our purpose is to produce college presidents." With his blessing, I walked out of his office a free man, ready to do the whole will of God and lead a Christian junior college into the ranks of fully accredited Christian liberal arts colleges.

Later, I learned that Dr. Henderson had counted on me to take his place as Interim Director so that he could take a leave to care for his wife who was dying of cancer. Even though he was an avowed agnostic, his sacrifice for me will forever be remembered as a genuine expression of love and grace. Cyrus, King of Persia, comes to mind. Even though he was a pagan despot, the Lord moved his heart to free the Israelites and build a temple in

Jerusalem (Isaiah 44:23–45:6). With great thanksgiving, we honor our sovereign Lord, knowing that He also warms the heart of those whom He uses to work His good will in us.

A VISION CONFIRMED

As the youngest college president in the nation, I began my work as President of Spring Arbor Junior College in 1961 with an immediate aim on advancement to a four-year institution. It was not an easy task. Because of my commitment to build a fully accredited, four-year Christian liberal arts college, I had to walk back some of the decisions that the former president had made. One instance stands out in my mind. A psychologist had been hired to teach third- and fourth-year courses in advance of accreditation. I had to go to her and rescind the offer. She responded with the threat of a formal lawsuit and followed with attempts to sabotage my character. As difficult as it was, we had to start with a clean slate on the development of an accredited senior college.

I see now how the Spirit of God led me into a holistic vision for Christian higher education. To begin, as I traced the history of my Wesleyan heritage, I sensed powerful motivation rising out of Charles Wesley's plea, "*Let us unite the pair so long disjoined/ Knowledge and vital piety.*"[1] These words became the driving force for a lifetime of being a champion for the integration of faith and learning. Soon after, I encountered the writings of Origen with his critical question, "*What has Jerusalem to do with Athens?*"[2] From the classroom of his Alexandrian school, he also championed the premise for the integration of faith and learning. In that premise I foresaw the purpose of Christian higher education, whether ancient or contemporary. From there I not only read the scholars who advanced the integrative principle, but also the texts of European and American history that traced the principle into curricular theory and practice.

1. Wesley, *Poetical Works*, 408.
2. Tertullian, *Prescription Against Heresies*, Chapter 7.

I also had the unusual opportunity to be personally mentored by seven of the greatest theologians, educators and statesmen of the twentieth century. One is Arthur Holmes, the Wheaton professor, whose classic text, *The Idea of the Christian College*, is grounded in the premise, "All truth is God's truth."[3]

Another is Bernard Ramm, the Reform theologian, who taught me a process for the integration of faith and learning. The third is Elton Trueblood, the Earlham philosopher, whose life motive is encapsuled in his declaration that, "A Christian is one who bets his life that Christ is right."[4] Fourth is John Stott, the All-Souls Rector in London, who challenged me to frame my faith as the integrating force in the social mission of Christian higher education. Fifth is Frank Gaberlein, the Stony Brook headmaster, who spelled out the meaning of wholeness in the curriculum of the Christian college. Sixth, is Lloyd Ogilvie, Chaplain of the U.S. Senate, with whom I shared the confidence of covenant brothers. Seventh and finally, I count Mark Hatfield, the United States senator, as my model for the holistic witness of our faith in the contemporary world. Indeed, I am a student most blessed.

THE BUCKEYE'S CALL

Shortly after my inauguration as President of Spring Arbor College, I received a surprise call from President Novice Fawcett of The Ohio State University. President Fawcett and I had become friends after I did the research for his office on the Trimester calendar option. Just before the meeting of the President's Cabinet when I would report the results of the study, I made the decision to move to the University of Michigan, the prime competitor in football against Ohio State. When President Fawcett introduced me to his Cabinet, he went through my credentials and then, with a wry smile, he said, "I am sorry to announce that McKenna is leaving us and going to Ann Arbor College."

---

3. Holmes, *Idea of a Christian College,* 7.
4. Trueblood, *New Man For Our Time,* 29.

I had no further contact with President Fawcett until the month after my inauguration at Spring Arbor. To my complete surprise, he made a personal phone call to me. With presidential demeanor he began our conversation with the memory of our relationship at Ohio State and then, with his patented crispness, he offered, "Dave, how would you like to be the President of Wright State University, a brand-new school in Dayton, Ohio? If you are interested, I can make sure that you get the job." His words overwhelmed a thirty-one-year-old kid in his first presidency. I knew that he was telling the truth. For good reason, the official name, "The Ohio State" told the whole story. Whoever was president of the University called the shots for all other public institutions of higher education in Ohio, including community colleges.

I didn't pause in my answer because I knew that I had been called of God to the presidency of Spring Arbor Junior College. After thanking him for his confidence, I said, "No, I cannot accept your offer because I am called to the presidency of Spring Arbor." Before I could go on, President Fawcett raised the question, "Dave, how much are you making there?" I answered, "$10,000." He was shocked and came back quickly with the unforgettable words, "TEN THOUSAND DOLLARS? I'm talking about $25,000 at Wright State and the sky's the limit." Needless to say, I felt honored by his offer, but without hesitation, I still said, "Thank you. I appreciate your confidence, but my decision is firm. I will stay at Spring Arbor."

I must confess that I am always curious to know about the road not traveled. If I had two lives, I might try the presidency of a public university, but I have never had a moment's doubt about making the right decision.

A MIRACLE MOMENT

My Spring Arbor years are remembered for the privilege of starting a new Christian liberal arts college. Faculty members were quick to respond to my challenge to create a general education curriculum to demonstrate the integration of faith and learning in every subject of the liberal arts. They responded by developing the Christian Perspective in the Liberal Arts curriculum (CPLA) with integration as the guiding principle for courses in the humanities, physical sciences, natural sciences, social sciences and religion. Our goal was to achieve recognition with the North Central Accrediting Association so that our graduates would be recognized and our students could transfer credits to another institution.

The process leading to regional accreditation had episodes ranging from border-line despair to unprecedented praise. To begin, we had determined that we could not go forward with the plan for the four-year college without the status of full accreditation. A major barrier stood in the way.

The NCAA required at least one graduating class from the four-year college to show that the purpose of the institution was being fulfilled. We had determined that we would not ask our students to graduate from an unaccredited college. Still, we began the demanding process of self-study, assessing our current strengths and weaknesses as well as projecting our plans for the future. After a full year of work, the study was complete, and we presented our findings and our plan to the NCAA Commission on Accreditation. The fact that no institution had been accredited as a four-year college without one graduating class stood in the way of success, but we felt as if we had a case that had to be heard.

With a team composed of vice-presidents and the director of the self-study, we met with the Commission on Accrediting at their headquarters in Chicago, Illinois. For the first four hours we presented our case. Another two hours involved in-depth discussion and critical questions regarding our case. The give-and-take was so intense that we left feeling exhausted and discouraged. When we arrived back at our hotel, we shared our dismay with each other and began to talk about options for the future of the college.

A telephone call from the Chair of the Commission interrupted our wake. On the other end of the line I heard the miraculous words, "Spring Arbor has been fully accredited as a four-year college with a follow-up self-study after the first graduating class." Our whoops could not be contained. Then, the Chair told us the story behind the story. We had put the construction of a new library at the center of our plans and as proof of our serious academic intent. Our case was weak because our prospect for funding was limited to a vague promise of a prospective donor. The Chair, however, reviewed the discussion of his Commission and the basis for their affirmative decision. He said the question hung in the balance until one of the Commission members, the President of Bowling Green University, said that he knew the prospective donor for our new library, Ray Herrick of Adrian, Michigan. In confidence he said, "I know the donor. I know that his word is good. Spring Arbor will get its library." On the basis of his report, we received full accreditation as a four-year Christian liberal arts college. Two years later, we dedicated the Ray Herrick Library and graduated our first baccalaureate class. Needless to say, this miraculous moment was the turning point for Spring Arbor and its progress from a junior college to a senior college and, later, to a university. A history of 150 years is highlighted by auspicious moments when the evidence of God's hand was graciously placed on Spring Arbor and its ongoing ministry. Among these moments, none is more memorable or more miraculous than the happenings behind the closed doors of the North Central Accrediting Commission.

The achievement of accreditation was not without its trauma. After we received accreditation, I found out that the bright young professor who directed the self-study had falsified his academic credentials. He not only counted himself among the limited number of Ph.Ds on our faculty but signed all of his correspondence with the false credential and dared to add the letters to the name on his office door. After I confronted and fired him, I had to decide what to do about our accredited status. Would the affirmative decision be rescinded because of the falsified credentials of the self-study director? I decided that I had to confront the question head-on. Making another trip to Chicago, I confessed the flaw in our self-study and pleaded my case before the Executive Director of North Central Regional Accreditation. He responded with understanding and compassion for a beleaguered young president. The error was noted, but accreditation was retained. We were back on track toward a fully accredited, four-year Christian liberal arts college.

AN IDEA MADE WHOLE

At the center of this story is the work of the board, administration, and faculty bonding together to frame a missional statement as the focus and motivation for our development as an accredited, four-year Christian liberal arts college. To assist us in our quest, we engaged Tom Jones, President of Earlham College, a prominent Quaker school, as our consultant. Tom's approach to his task was unique. When he arrived on campus, he took it upon himself to pose a gutsy question to every segment of the College—board members, administrators, faculty, and students as well as staff members and the alumni board. "What's the big idea?" His query prompted us to put aside the standard statements of institutional mission and led us to pose a vision that revolutionized the campus and fired our imagination for the future. Believe it or not, the mission statement proposed for the future of Spring Arbor College was conceived while we were riding backward in the rear seat of the College station wagon and travelling at 70 miles an hour on I-90 between Chicago and Spring Arbor. Out of that speeding vehicle, the Spring Arbor Concept was born:

> *Spring Arbor University is a community of learners distinguished by our life-long involvement in the study and application of the liberal arts, total commitment to Jesus Christ as the perspective for learning, and critical participation in the contemporary world.*[5]

Many mission statements come and go on the tide of academic ideas and current events. The Spring Arbor Concept is the exception. Sixty-three years after its formal acceptance as the mission statement for Spring Arbor University, The Concept is still the clear and guiding vision for the school. In fact, during a recent visit by a regional accrediting team, the members of the team made a

---

5. *A Concept to Keep*, 175.

special note in their report citing the fact that our students could state The Concept and spell out its meaning. If I were asked to name the major contribution that I have made to Christian higher education, I would cite the privilege of leading the community in the development and application of The Spring Arbor Concept. To God be the glory!

****

SEEING ALL THINGS WHOLE *THE BIG IDEA*

The Big Idea lives on. During the years that followed full accreditation for the Christian liberal arts college, the question was whether or not The Big Idea could be translated into the lives of people and the viability of programs. Three pivotal points stand out as tests for the potency of The Big Idea in its application through The Spring Arbor Concept.

A SENSE OF BELONGING

The first pivotal point is the sense of belonging in a community of learners. As I reflected earlier, it was the sense of belonging that made the most impression on me as a college freshman back in 1947. Even though I knew no one on campus and had to witness ready-made groups from the Free Methodist Conference, the "spirit of the place" took me in as a full member of the family. Most importantly, the experience of community was transforming. Whether in classes, chapel, concerts, or athletic contests, the tone of the campus had a profound effect on its students. Of course, the power of transformation was conveyed through the witness of faculty who lived out the meaning of the "community of learners." When we were framing The Concept a debate took place around the question, "Should we add 'scholars' after 'learners' in order to include the faculty?" The proposed change was lost because the faculty wanted it made clear that they were "learners" along with their students. One can readily sense what it means when we talk about "belonging" and "transformation" for the Spring Arbor community.

THE CENTER FOR LEARNING

A second pivotal point is "…total commitment to Jesus Christ as the perspective for learning." The faculty meeting where this phrase was vigorously debated is still fresh in my mind. At issue was whether the statement would read "**the** perspective for learning" or "**a** perspective for learning." Those who wanted The Concept to read, "**a** perspective for learning" argued that liberal learning required the exploration of multiple perspectives, of which the Christian viewpoint was one. They agreed that they would still come down on the side of the Christian perspective, but not until other options had been explored. Faculty who took the side of "**the** perspective for learning" contended that all teachers bring a viewpoint to their subject, a viewpoint that effects their presentation of other viewpoints. Therefore, Christian scholars are defined by the fact that they are "totally committed to Jesus Christ as **the** perspective for learning." Their case was clear and "**the**" won the day. You can see the impact of that decision in the titles of core courses in the Christian Perspective in the Liberal Arts:[6]

> **Core 100**—Discovery in the Liberal Arts through a community of learners
>
> **Core 200**—Involvement in the Christian faith: Issues and Cultures
>
> **Core 274 and 275**—Critical Participation in the contemporary world outside one's own culture
>
> **Core 300**—Discovering the Christian Faith: Its practices through Jesus Christ as the perspective for learning
>
> **Core 400**—The Christian in the contemporary world

6. *Keeping the Concept*, 74–75.

To finalize these learning experiences, a Senior Capstone course was required of each student. The purpose of the course was to have the senior student write a paper exploring the integration of faith and learning in his or her major field. I, as president, had a cadre of six students who presented and defended their papers before me. Out of that experience, I recall the senior who concluded our session by saying, "Now I know what Christian higher education is all about." Her words confirmed the fact that I felt as if the moment was also the capstone for my teaching career. Without doubt, the investment of the Spring Arbor faculty in creative and Christian curriculum development is more than a credit to their work. It stands tall among both Christian and secular schools who claim to be centers for liberal learning.

THE RISK OF WITNESS

The final pivotal point is the application of the phrase *"Critical participation in the contemporary world."* Contrary to the expectations of some, "critical participation" is not a license for condemning the contemporary world. Yes, Christians will have to be a prophetic minority in a society that is no friend to grace. Note also that every recommendation for Christian living as a prophetic minority is positive in its approach. This does not rule out the quality of Spirit-guided discernment in addressing the culture and deciding on action. Christians do have something to say and should say it.

If I were asked how the meaning of "critical participation" has changed since its inception in 1960, I would emphasize "risk-taking" and "sacrifice" as nuances to be considered. Full credit needs to be given for the risks that we took during our tenure at Spring Arbor. Leading the way was the "riot scholarships" that were given to Black youth whose opportunity for college was burned in the riots of Detroit in 1967. To bring seven young men from their impoverished setting and out of urban violence on to a campus known as the "quiet cove of the Spirit" is a risk of risks. Yet, we did it without disaster and with qualified academic results.

Perhaps most important was the fact that "riot scholarships" at Spring Arbor gave the incentive for the Michigan legislature to pass a bill for Opportunity Grants to fund other students from impoverished settings in the private colleges and universities of the state.

Another example of risk-taking back in the 1960's was the conference sponsored by Spring Arbor under the title of "The Urban Crisis." Looking back upon that event now brings shivers to the spine. Imagine little Spring Arbor in its village setting hosting such notaries as Jerome Cavanaugh, Mayor of Detroit, Hubert Locke, from the Office of Religious Affairs at Wayne State University, and Francis Keppel, President of the General Learning Corporation (formerly, United States Commissioner of Education) on the campus for three days of unfettered discussion of the crisis facing our cities across the nation. Add to the ranks of public officials the names of scholars David Moberg, Chair of Social Sciences at Bethel College, and Mario DiGangi, from the Bible and Missionary Fellowship. To say the least, the mix was potent. No issue was dodged and no responsibilities were short-changed. As president, in closing the conference, I dared to ask our students,

> "Do we have the will, the commitment, and the grace to run the risk in what Harvey Cox calls, 'God's floating crap game?'
>
> Norman Vincent Peale has written, 'You can play it cool and you will freeze, or you can play it hot and you may get burned, but at least you will shed some warmth over a discouraged and bewildered world.'" **I dare you to play it hot.**[7]

At the center of this message is the challenge for Spring Arbor students to participate in the contemporary world, not just at risk, but at self-sacrifice. It is a challenge that still hangs in the air more than 50 years later. Without risking the sacrifice of self-interest there can be neither holiness nor wholeness.

7. McKenna, *The Urban Crisis*, 142

6

Seattle Pacific University
Roots and Shoots

MY COMMITMENT TO DO the whole will of God came to another test after seven years of tenure at Spring Arbor College. Having achieved the goal of a fully-accredited Christian liberal arts college in 1967, we received an invitation to the presidency of Seattle Pacific College in Seattle, Washington. If we accepted the position, it meant a transcontinental move from a small village in Michigan to a metropolis in the Northwest. We were faced with another win-win decision. Our success at Spring Arbor gave us full confidence for a future of leadership in Christian higher education. Seattle Pacific College, however, represented a significant step up in scope and scale, with its reputation in the Christian liberal arts as well as professional studies.

A STEP OF FAITH

Jan and I weighed our options. She was pregnant with our fourth child and a transcontinental move would come right after our second son's birth. Also, Jan's aging parents had retired from the itinerant ministry and settled in Spring Arbor, just a few blocks from our home. They loved to babysit and would be a special help for Jan after the birth of her baby. To their everlasting credit, Jan's parents remembered how the call of God took them from parish to parish during their ministerial days. In keeping with that commitment, even though it hurt, they urged us to follow the will of God. If it meant a move to Seattle, they would understand.

Once again, the call of God became clear for us. We accepted the presidency of Seattle Pacific College and made the move in July, 1968, five weeks after the birth of our son, Robert Bruce. Once again, Jan confirmed her role among pioneer women who followed their husbands into the frontier. In addition to a new baby, we had three other children to adjust into new schools and a half-finished president's home where Jan had to rock Rob as carpenters and painters scurried from room to room.

A BANKER'S CALL

While we were adjusting to the new environment and two weeks before I officially took office, I received a call from the President of the National Bank of Commerce. He informed me that Seattle Pacific College was in financial trouble, so much so that our line of credit would no longer be honored. The news came as a complete shock to the Board of Trustees as well as to me. We soon learned that the vice-president for finance had cleverly juggled funds in order to hide the mounting debt. Seattle Pacific College had a sterling reputation for paying its debts until the crisis of 1968. At that time, we were racing toward bankruptcy with not enough money to pay our faculty and our creditors. As president, I took on the responsibility to meet with creditors and ask for a deferral until we got our house in order. The reputation of the College paid off and we got some breathing room for reworking our budget and erasing our debts. To begin, we engaged the services of Touche-Ross accountants to do a complete audit of our books. After a period of time, they came back shaking their heads and saying, "The books are so bad, we cannot solve the problem. It is best to start over with a new financial benchmark."

A FIRST LADY'S FAITH

When I got the news of pending bankruptcy, I asked God why He called me to Seattle Pacific College. I was especially concerned about Jan as she juggled the needs of three growing children and a new baby. Several weeks went by, while I kept the news from her. Finally, I knew that I had no choice. I had to break the news to her. Choosing our favorite coffee shop across the Washington ship canal, I took her to lunch and told her the full story. At the end I said, "Honey, we have a choice. Because we did not know about the financial condition before we made our decision, we can stay at the risk of failure or leave and start over." Jan's lifetime of moving with her parents from parish to parish and following the will of God informed her response. She looked at me with eyes full of resolve and said, "Did God call us to Seattle Pacific?" I answered, "Yes, there is no doubt about it." Without a moment's hesitation she declared, "Well, if so, what are we waiting for? Let's go."

Jan joins so many women of faith who have both supported and led their husbands on the faith journey. Her words set me on a course of leadership with financial integrity as our highest priority. A balanced budget was our primary goal. But first, we had to cover the debts that came close to ruining us. As an example, our debt to the Federal government for construction of new buildings, including Demaray Hall where the president's office was located, put on us an onerous burden of regular payments. Desperation took me to Washington, D.C to meet Housing and Urban Development officials and ask for temporary relief from our burden. Graciously, they heard our plight and granted a deferral. Four years later I returned to Washington to meet with the HUD people again. This time I took with me the word that we were now ready to resume our payments and make up the deferred funds. The HUD administrator who had heard our plan responded with astonishment. He said, "I have had to grant deferrals to many institutions across the nation, but you are first one in my experience who has come back saying that you are ready to resume payments on your building loan."

A CULTURAL CHALLENGE

Our outcome with the new financial plan and a fund-raising campaign brought us back to balanced budget in four years. My first thought was that we could now return to my primary strength in long-range strategic planning built around a vision for the future with emphasis on the integration of faith and learning in a Christian liberal arts curriculum. I soon learned the difference between starting a new institution, as we did at Spring Arbor, and inheriting an organization and curriculum long-established and deeply engrained. Even more significantly, I realize now that we had changed worlds – from the "quiet cove of the Spirit" in Spring Arbor, Michigan to the teeming urban culture of Seattle, Washington. The topography defines the difference. In the flatland of the Mid-West people come together in groups; in the mountainous land of the Northwest the individual reigns. This difference is reinforced by the pioneering spirit and the recency of settlements for the Pacific Northwest. Seattle Pacific University is a case in point. The school was not only founded by pioneers who made their way West, but its future was assured by Free Methodists from the Midwest, such as Kansas, who wanted to escape the confines of conformity in the Midwestern flatlands. It is important to understand this difference because it bears directly on the outcome of leadership with an agenda for wholeness of community around a common mission.

A VISION PROJECTED

For the opening convocation in 1970, I dared to speak on the subject, "A Vision of Wholeness" based on the questions, "Who are we? and "Why are we here?" In this speech I dared to propose three operating principles for wholeness:

1. "All truth is potentially Whole Truth;"

2. "Every individual is potentially a Whole Person;" and

3. "Every act of service is potentially a Whole World."

The speech was well-accepted, but reality ruled. General education at Seattle Pacific was a series of uncoordinated courses with ready substitutions that students could make. Moreover, the academic departments tended to be silos of content and management that defied revolutionary change. Because of the financial obligations that pressed upon us, I could only present the case of "A Vision of Wholeness" without the time or energy to implement it. Even though I pressed home my mantra, "See the Vision, State the mission, and Set the tone" in every chapel talk I gave, the best that I could do for the first eight years of my tenure was to balance the budget and project forward a university status for the institution.

A DISCONTENT'S DISAPPOINTMENT

Throughout my career in higher education, I was always intrigued by options that were presented to me in academic and Christian leadership. Looking back, I wonder whether my interest in new positions was driven by an exaggerated ego or by creative vision. There is another alternative. Was God showing me the kingdoms of the educational and Christian world as temptation in order to test my spiritual resolve? If so, the question is not whether I was tempted but whether I answered, "Get thee behind me, Satan, thou shall worship the Lord your God and Him only shall you serve." Let me give an example.

In 1977, Jan and I took a European vacation. Our travels led us to the French Rivera, Monaco, and Holiday Inn on the Mediterranean Sea. On our first trip to the beach, we heard a sunbather say, "Did you see him? Billy Graham is over there." Following their gaze, I saw Billy hiding behind a floppy hat and dark glasses. Ruth, his wife, sat next to him almost in full dress. Because of our past association, I felt free to walk over to them, and behind my dark glasses, ask in a fake accent, "Meester Graham, may I have your autograph?' A look of surprise crossed Billy's face and he quickly blew my cover, "Dave McKenna, what are you doing here?"

For the next three days, we shared a beach with Billy and Ruth. On the second day, they invited Jan and me to dinner at a restaurant high on the Upper Cornish. Of course, we accepted and began to prepare for the event. I took Jan uptown to buy a new dress and I made sure that I was wearing my best summer pants and shirt. But, when we met Billy and Ruth in the lobby, we realized that we were overdressed. Billy had on an outfit that is best described as fatigues with a flair and Ruth wore a very simple summer dress.

Our dinner that night is one to remember. A table was ordered back in a corner to give the Grahams their privacy with Jan and me seated to block the viewpoint of other guests. High on the Upper Cornish over the Mediterranean Sea, we feasted on the fresh offerings from a farm of renown. Billy and Ruth excelled in the way that they made two awe-stricken kids feel special. On the way back to our motel, Billy began to talk about *Christianity Today*, the periodical that he founded and where Carl Henry, the noted theologian, had just retired as Editor-in-Chief. After reflecting on Carl's retirement and the search for his replacement, Billy said, "Dave, we thought about you as editor, but you are doing such a good job at Seattle Pacific, we didn't want to take you away." Like an overinflated balloon that got punctured and all the air escaped, I gasped in disbelief. To be editor-in-chief of *Christianity Today* was my dream and my work at Seattle Pacific had come to a pause. Of course, I said nothing until Jan and I were alone in our room. Together, we asked what God was trying to tell us. After a long conversation, we decided that God was saying again, "Dave, I called you to Seattle Pacific. You have seen My hand at work in a dramatic turnaround. Now, it is time to be faithful." The lesson has never been forgotten. God not only calls us to visionary ventures, He calls us to be faithful.

Oh yes, on that trip to Monaco, I also discovered a bit of Billy's humanity. He and I were floating together in the Mediterranean Sea and gabbing about little things until Billy said, "I don't dare let anyone know that we are here. If Princess Grace knew that we were here, she would want us to stay with her in the Pink Palace." Gulp! I had a glimpse of the same fascination with fame over which I felt convicted. I had heard the heartbeat of a kid from the hills of North Carolina and my respect for him took a giant leap. My hero was human!

Don't get me wrong. I have never doubted for a moment that Billy Graham was anointed of God as His witness for 20th-century Christianity. My conviction was confirmed at the 1976 World Congress on Evangelism in Lausanne, Switzerland. After the conference sessions during the day, Billy preached each night at an evangelistic rally in the local sports stadium. On the first night, we learned that Billy had been sick throughout the day but still insisted on preaching at night. I sat in a stadium seat just above the rostrum from which Billy would preach. When the time came for the sermon, Billy made his way to the pulpit, leaned on it and began to preach in a husky voice. Soon, a gust of wind swept some of his notes off the desk and he began to shuffle the papers trying to find his place. Finally, after relying on past preaching, he cut the sermon short and gave an invitation to his hearers to accept Christ. From every indication, the evening was doomed to disaster. But when I looked up and across the soccer field toward the crowd in the stands, I saw scores of persons filing down the stairs and onto the field. More than 300 seekers were identified as converts that night. For those who are skeptics, a follow-up study was done years later on those who professed Christ that night and the findings astounded the investigators. A high percentage of the converts continued in the faith and shared their witness. As for me, a bit skeptical myself, I never again doubted that Billy Graham was God's chosen instrument for the evangelical witness of our time.

THE UNIVERSITY MODEL

Seattle Pacific's location in Seattle with the University of Washington just a few blocks away and Seattle University just across town carried its own challenge. With a bit of derision, we were usually identified as "The Little School by the Canal." So, after getting our financial house in order we began to review the options for future development. A select liberal arts college did not appear feasible because it would require complete deconstruction and reconstruction of a curriculum in both undergraduate and graduate studies that were already leaning toward a university structure. Even more important, we asked how best we could expand our evangelical Christian witness in the city and beyond. So, after receiving a grant from The Battelle Institute in Seattle for the specific purpose of visioning and developing a university model, representatives of the board, administration and faculty met for three days to think, speak, and pray over our future. The outcome was a master plan with strategic initiatives for the creation of Seattle Pacific University. At the following Board meeting, the plan was approved, and the university was born.

The university decision had sweeping implications for mission, structure, and outcomes along with major financial implications. Having come from debt to a balanced budget the new challenge was in fund-raising for new buildings, advanced programs, faculty support and scholarships. The city of Seattle, of course, was our opportunity as well as our challenge. No extended capital campaign took place during my Seattle tenure, but fund-raising was an ongoing task. For example, when we recycled the old railroad barn for a science center, my time was consumed by calls upon prospective donors and foundations. With past years of debt still in mind, we determined that we would build and rebuild without incurring a financial burden once again. True to this premise, we were able to build the science center, the school of business, a new gym adjoining Brougham Arena, and a bank-bookstore at the entrance to campus as well as remodel other facilities and purchase properties for future expansion without going into debt. In each case, we counted on our contacts in the greater Seattle area for initial funding. Our competition was not only the University of Washington, but Seattle University, the Jesuit school just across town. Father William O'Sullivan, President of Seattle University, and I were fast friends despite the fact that our footsteps frequently crossed in our fund-raising efforts. Later, when I announced that I was leaving Seattle Pacific University for Asbury Theological Seminary, Father O'Sullivan conferred upon me an honorary doctorate in recognition of our common spirit and success. After conferring the degree upon me, he quipped, "This is how you handle competition. Now, the city is all mine." His words were true, but not with rancor. Father Bill, as I knew him, was paying me the highest of compliments.

THE TAPROOT OF HISTORY

Out of my experience as a college president, I developed the working principle for dealing with institutional crisis: "Dig for the roots, prune the shoots." Institutions get in trouble when they forget either their history or their discipline. Seattle Pacific University is an example. Even before the university model was complete with its strategic discipline, we were also digging for the roots that anchored the institution in its history and purpose.

As its taproot in history, Seattle Pacific University is anchored in the missionary motive of its founders. While foreign missions held its attention, the local mission field of Seattle, a burgeoning metropolis, continued to test the institution and its founding purpose. Urban Seattle in the late 1990's and early 2000's had a reputation as a rough and ready pioneering outpost specializing in lumber and fishing as well as booze, prostitution, and gambling. First Avenue along the waterfront got nicknamed "Skid Row" as a way to describe the logs that were sluiced down the street on their way to the mill. The name got its negative connotation from the bars, brothels, and gambling parlors along the way. Soon, Skid Row became the name for similar streets of degradation across the nation. Seattle, however, had the dubious distinction of a pioneering mentality that caused the lumberjacks and fisherman to quip, "Who are you running from?"

GRACE FOR A CITY

Despite the handicap of a hostile urban climate, a miracle of grace took place in the 1930's and 1940's. Abraham Vereide, a tough-minded Norwegian, determined to bring the message and spirit of Christ to a sinful city.[1] He established in Seattle what became the national Prayer Breakfast movement and later, International Christian Leadership. Personal spirituality was matched with social responsibility in the message of Vereide. Out of prayer breakfasts came a mayor of Seattle and a governor of Washington, both dedicated Christians with an agenda of spiritual and moral reformation for their beloved city and state. As further expression of Vereide's faith, the Good Will industry was founded as a vehicle for giving work to the homeless along with the opportunity to share the Christian message. In sum, Abraham Vereide and his companions in Christ saw Seattle transformed from a city known for its sin and corruption to one of the best places in the world to live.

Seattle Pacific Seminary, then College, was a vital part of spiritual reform in its home city. Located on Queen Anne hill just a breath away from downtown, the school has a history that centers in men and women who gave themselves unstintingly to the cause of Christ on the American frontier. After treks across the country and bumping up against the Pacific Ocean, it was natural that missionary ventures pointed to the Orient and all points West.

A MISSIONARY MOTIVE

Symbolizing the missionary spirit of Seattle Pacific College, and now University, is the name of Jacob DeShazer. He had his claim to fame as an airman with the Dolittle raiders who dared to attack the mainland of Japan before the tide of the Pacific theater of war turned in favor of the United States. DeShazer's B-24 bomber went down over China, but the crew bailed out only to survive as prisoners in a Japanese concentration camp. It was there that Jake DeShazer found a Bible and gave his heart to Jesus Christ. He was released after the surrender of Japan and returned home to the highest accolades and as a recipient of medals of honor and

---

1. Grubb, *Modern Viking*.

freedom bestowed by the President of the United States. Books were written and movies screened in honor of him and his heroism. Even more profound, DeShazer brought home a heart of love for the Japanese people. As a member of the Free Methodist Church, he chose Seattle Pacific College as the school of choice for his preparation as a missionary to Japan. After graduation, he was quick to pack his bags and return to Japan with his family. Although his oratorical skills were limited, DeShazer's story of forgiveness made him one of the most effective of Free Methodist missionaries.

In 1980, Jan and I led the Seattle Pacific University choir and a cadre of alumni to Japan as an expression of our continuing commitment to the vision of missions on which the school was founded. Jake DeShazer was our humble, soft-spoken host whose spirit spoke loud and clear. When we returned home, I determined to reprint the book that President C. Hoyt Watson had authored under the title *The Amazing Story of Sgt. Jacob DeShazer.*[2] The book still lives today with its captivating story of Jacob DeShazer's ministry. I especially remember the moment when the Dolittle raider shared the platform of an evangelistic crusade with Mitsuo Fuchida, commander of the Kamikaze pilots at Pearl Harbor. True to the Gospel message, the former enemies embraced and then each gave his testimony of faith in Jesus Christ. For good reason, Jacob DeShazer is remembered as an alumnus who represents the highest and best of vision, mission and tone for Seattle Pacific University.

AN INCREDIBLE TRIO

The reputation of Seattle Pacific College (University) opened up unusual opportunities for leadership both in Seattle and on the national scene. In 1978, I served as Secretary for the National Association of Independent Colleges and Universities (NAICU). Primary to our purpose was to assure religious freedom for

2. Watson, *Story of Sargeant Jacob DeShazer,* 1963.

faith-based schools in their hiring practices. This meant defining or eliminating "religion" from the Equal Employment Opportunities Commission's regulations against race, color, religion, sex, national origin, disability or age discrimination in hiring practices. To represent the interests of NAICU, Dallin Oaks, President of Brigham Young University, James Burtchell, Provost of the University of Notre Dame, and I, President of Seattle Pacific University joined together to carry our case with the EEOC Commission. Unusual bedfellows, indeed. A Mormon, a Roman Catholic, and an Evangelical bonded together to champion the cause for a religious exemption that would permit us to hire only members for administration, faculty and staff positions who shared the faith position of the hiring institution. I count those days among the best of my career, not just because we won our case for the religious exemption, but because of the privilege of being colleagues and friends with President Oaks and Provost Burchtell. As a result of our work behind the scenes all faith-based institutions in the nation gained the privilege of hiring only persons who shared the religious position of the parent school. Although there have been multiple contests and court cases attempting to change the provision, the exemption still holds as one of the guardrails for religious freedom in American higher education.

MY BEST SPEECH

In 1980, Senator Mark Hatfield nominated me as Secretary of Education in the Reagan Cabinet. When I asked what I could do to support his nomination, he answered, "Nothing. If God is in it, it will be." So I waited for weeks, watching all of the news announcing Cabinet positions. Nothing came through related to the Secretary of Education. Finally, the leader of the Republican party in the State of Washington decided to take the matter into own hands, travel to Washington, and present my name personally to Vice-President George Herbert Walker Bush. Another period of waiting followed and then the headline came, "Terrell Bell, Secretary of Higher Education for the State of Utah, named Secretary of Education by President Reagan." Needless to say, I was shocked and disappointed.

Later, I learned that my name was among the finalists, but the political power of the Mormon Church won out. According to confidential sources, Bill Mariott, CEO of hotel fame, called the President and said, "We didn't get our man in Labor. We didn't get our man in Commerce. We want our man in Education." Or course, Mormon power won out and Terrell Bell was named Secretary. When I heard this news, I remembered Senator Hatfield saying, "If God is in it, it will be." Reluctantly, I tried to accept the fact that the position was not in God's will for me.

On my next trip to Washington, I met with Senator Hatfield and spun out the story of my disappointment. He listened patiently and then said, "I know how you feel. Let me share a bit of my story with you. At the Republican national convention in 1968, I was to be nominated to run for the Vice-Presidency with Richard Nixon. On the evening before the final vote of the delegation, my wife and I had such confidence in the results that we went to bed early. The next morning, we awakened to the news that, sometime in the middle of the night, the expected decision was reversed and Spiro Agnew was named as the vice-presidential candidate."

Senator Hatfield's revelation overwhelmed me. I was sitting with the man who should have been the President of the United States after Nixon resigned! With the same calm and steady voice, the Senator said, "It took a long time to work through my disappointment, but because I had prayed that God's will be done, I now accept that decision even though I will always wonder what I would have done as President. Dave, I know how you feel." I could only feel ashamed for pouting over my loss of the position as Secretary of Education. Senator Hatfield served as God's agent to help me accept God's will and go forward.

I flew home just in time for the Homecoming weekend at Seattle Pacific. Events concluded with the Homecoming basketball game against our archrival, the University of Puget Sound, in the Seattle Center arena. Tradition called for me to greet the alumni and guests as the conclusion of half-time activities. Vividly now,

I remember walking up to the microphone knowing that our audience was well aware of the happenings of the past week. What would I say? After a sweeping look over the clapping crowd, I was inspired to speak, "I would rather be your president than his secretary." No further words were needed. The cheering confirmed the shortest speech I ever gave. With a wave I turned and walked back to my seat. It was not only a moment to remember. It was the shortest and best speech I ever gave. Most of all, it was a lesson taught by the Spirit of God. Even though I am a slow, slow learner, at least I learned my lesson. With eternal patience, He had led me step by step into His good and perfect will. Like C.S. Lewis, I came into the Kingdom "kicking and screaming."

****

SEEING ALL THINGS WHOLE
ROOTS AND SHOOTS

As I REFLECT UPON our years in the presidency at Seattle Pacific, the financial crisis of 1968 stands out as a learning experience that defines my leadership throughout the rest of my career. In the startup years of Spring Arbor College, I led by presidential pronouncements as much as by faculty planning sessions. As already noted, at Seattle Pacific I inherited a mature organization with the lines of authority fixed by time and tradition. Presidential pronouncements were received with a yawn and the attitude "these too shall pass." Not only did I have to learn how to work within the system, but to ask questions rather than make pronouncements and gain the confidence of the faculty by building relationships rather than assuming ready-made loyalty. As already noted, I learned to "dig for the roots and prune the shoots." Seattle Pacific has deep roots in visionary leadership and the taproot of the missionary motive. The leader's task is to dig for these roots and the vitality of saving faith that they represent. At the same time, the leader cannot sidestep the tougher task of pruning the shoots of extraneous programs and practices that extend the scope and scale of university expectations. How well I remember the decision that I had to make in the financial crisis of 1968 when I had to cut varsity tennis (the love of my life) because of excessive travels costs needed to play quality competition. The same discipline was needed to prune academic programs and auxiliary practices that tend to grow in a complex organization. In each case, I avoided the trap of getting engulfed in details. Instead, my approach was to return to my mantra for presidential leadership: See the Vision, State the Mission and Set the Tone. From this base, then, I created an agenda with priorities for presidential action. Whether in times of calm or crisis, these working principles still serve me as a guidance system for setting and resetting the direction of an institution.

1. To **See a Vision** that is grounded in Biblical truth and projected with inspired promise.

2. To **State a Mission** that fulfills purpose in a comprehensive strategy designed to integrate faith and learning as well as develop character and competence.

3. To **Set a Tone** of communal trust in which communication is open and conflict is resolved in a climate conducive to redemption.

These working principles do not stand alone. Each one is couched within a commitment to the whole will of God and with a prayer for His presence during the times that try our souls. They are also written with the confidence that an institution such as Seattle Pacific University is a "vine of God's own planting" with the taproot of faith and the branches of fruit that define its past and assure its future.

7

Asbury Theological Seminary
The Loop Is Closed

GOD HAD ONE MORE stop for us in Christian higher education. In 1982, we received the invitation to the presidency of Asbury Theological Seminary, our alma mater. After meeting with the Board of the Seminary, I turned down the generous offer conveyed to me by the Chair, Dr. Ira Gallaway. Later the same night, I had a long-distance call from James Earl Massey, a renowned preacher and member of the Asbury Board. James started the conversation by saying, "David, the Lord has been speaking to me. He wants you to be the president of Asbury." I retorted, "James, you have been talking with Ira." "No," he answered, "I have only been talking to the Lord." I was spellbound. What could I say? The next day I called Dr. Gallaway and accepted the invitation.

WORLD WESLEYAN LEADERSHIP

I brought to Asbury a holistic vision for World Wesleyan Leadership. Under the aegis *The Whole Bible for the Whole World*, the Seminary had an excellent reputation, but its vision for leadership seemed to be limited by its location in the village of Wilmore,

Kentucky. Early in my Asbury tenure, we began the work toward a mission statement that saw the vision, stated the mission, and set the tone for the future of the Seminary. We also developed a strategy for planning, implementing and accessing the curricular, co-curricular, and extra-curricular initiatives of a master plan. Work on the mission statement continued over a series of years and under successive presidents. Today, the statement is complete and serves as the touchstone for communication of the purpose of the Seminary. It reads,

> *Asbury Theological Seminary is a community called to prepare theologically educated, sanctified, Spirit-filled men and women to evangelize and to spread scriptural holiness throughout the world through the love of Jesus Christ, in the power of the Holy Spirit, and to the glory of God the Father.*

In these well-chosen words, we see again the triad of my working model for presidential leadership:

1. the **Vision** of a *"community called;"*

2. the **Mission** *"to evangelize and to spread scriptural holiness throughout the world;"* and

3. the **Tone** of *"theologically educated, sanctified, Spirit-filled men and women."*

A REVIVAL SPIRIT

The Asbury mission statement is more than a rhetorical construct. In the Asbury revivals of 1970 and 2023, the mission has come alive in the hearts, minds, and souls of students at both Asbury University and Asbury Theological Seminary. I have been a beneficiary of these outpourings as a president and a participant. As president of the Seminary, I became part of a community always ready for an awakening of the Holy Spirit. As president of Seattle Pacific University, I saw the stirrings on our campus of the 1970 Asbury revival. Chapel services ran throughout the night, skeptical students were anointed, and our witness extended to the streets of Seattle, where University of Washington students were in violent protest. These personal experiences leave no doubt. The Asbury revivals are genuine because of men and women who are witnesses to holiness and wholeness in their own personal Pentecost.

With anticipation of another Spirit-filled awakening, we began our presidency of the Seminary in 1982. For my inaugural address we advanced a program based on the vision, mission, and tone of World Wesleyan Leadership. First among North American seminaries, we received a grant that permitted us to bring to campus a satellite station by which we telecast inaugural events across North America and even into Europe. My vision, however, bumped up against a prior commitment of the Board of Trustees to establish the E. Stanley Jones School of World Mission and Evangelism. I made an appeal for time to design the school, initiate funding, and relate its development to strategic planning for the whole Seminary. The faculty, in particular, opposed the decision because they saw it as taking funds away from existing programs and shifting emphasis from the core programs in theology to missions and evangelism. The Board, however, rejected my appeal in no uncertain terms and I was left with a questionable mandate and a disgruntled faculty. Obviously, these issues raised questions about the call of God to Asbury. They directly countered the way in which I envisioned leadership of the Seminary.

CALL AND RELEASE

As might be expected, I began to look around for an escape. I recall interviews for positions with foundations, an accrediting agency, and a global venture in missions. None of these options provided me with an escape. Finally, the offer of a lifetime came to me. The Consortium of Christian Colleges, of which I was Founding Chair of the Board, offered me the role as President and Executive Director. To back up the invitation, the current Chair conveyed the message of the Board, "Here is a blank check. Fill in the numbers."

How could the offer be refused? It brought together my vision, my leadership gifts and my academic strengths.

Once again, Jan and I went to prayer to get God's clearance for the decision, even though it was already fixed in our minds. Before finalizing my response, I asked counsel of my friend and colleague, George Brushaber, President of Bethel College and Seminary in St. Paul, Minnesota. George was a member of the Consortium Board and wanted me to accept the position. Yet, he sensed some hesitation that prompted him to say, "God not only calls us to a position, He releases us from the position. We have called you. Has God released you?"

George struck a nerve that sent shudders down my spine. Yes, I was called to Asbury, but had I been released? After new seasons of prayer, the answer was clear. God had not released me from the presidency of Asbury. Resolve mixed with disappointment brought me to the decision. I declined the invitation and went back to the difficult and demanding task of leadership at the Seminary.

GOD'S CONFIRMATION

Two years later, I saw why God had not released me from the Seminary. A call came from a man named Willian Conger, a retired Army colonel, who introduced himself as the executor for the estate of Ralph and Orlean Beeson, long-time donors to the Seminary and close friends with Dr. J.C. McPheeters, second President of the Seminary. Over several decades, Dr. McPheeters nurtured his friendship with the Beesons, resulting in significant grants to the Seminary for scholarships and missionary housing. Bill Conger, as he became known to us, said that after Ralph Beeson asked him to be his executor, he did a confidential check on Asbury with the local United Methodist Church pastor. When asked about Asbury, the pastor answered, "I don't know much about the Seminary, but one thing is certain, their graduates can preach." The pastor's commendation became the touchstone from which Bill Conger said, "I want to make Asbury a war college for preachers." He and I then developed a plan for funding a Chair of Biblical Preaching as well as outreach in educational technology and leadership initiatives, including the E. Stanley Jones School of World Mission and Evangelism. When the guidelines were clear, the announcement went out, "*The estate of Ralph and Orlean Beeson will fund the largest grant ever given to a free-standing theological seminary in American history.*" The announcement marked the beginning of a story that speaks of God's astounding grace. With the Beeson gift leading the way, the Asbury Seminary endowment has risen from $7 million in 1982 to $195 million in 2023, the Centennial year. I served just at the start of this record-breaking rise. My colleagues in the presidency who followed me – Maxie Dunnam, Jeffrey Greenway, Ellsworth Kalas, and Timothy Tennant – are all members of a presidential team that not only kept alive the momentum of the Beeson gift but also saw significant gifts added during the time of their administration. Credit also goes to the Board of Trustees for their wise stewardship of the endowment funds. As for me, I now apologize to God for doubting His calling and give thanks that He hadn't released me.

THE SABBATICAL TEST

Of all the lessons that I learned during my years in the administration of Christian higher education, one stands out. After seven years as President at Asbury Theological Seminary, the Board granted me a six-month sabbatical for writing and renewal. In preparation for my departure, I asked Robert Mulholland, our provost, if he would assume the role of chief executive officer during my absence. He readily concurred. Two or three briefing meetings were held when we reviewed pending executive matters, especially for the annual Board of Trustees meeting that would be held during my absence. With full confidence, then, Jan and I flew to Seattle, Washington, to stay in the ground floor apartment of our son's home and pursue the writing of a commentary on Isaiah.

Shortly after our arrival in Seattle, I received an urgent call from Sheila Lovell, my Executive Assistant at Asbury. Even though she had been fully briefed on the sabbatical plans and had an excellent working relationship with the interim president, she spoke with alarm, "Dr. Mulholland has just moved into your office and has taken over your desk. What should I do?"

My first reaction echoed the plaintive plea of Little Wee Bear in the story of Goldilocks, "Somebody's been sitting in my chair." Because Bob and I had not talked about the place from which he would serve as interim president I felt threatened by his action. So, I told Sheila that I would think about it and then speak to Bob. While trying to decide on how to approach the conversation, I remembered a fact that changed the whole complexion of the pending conversation. Robert Mulholland was not only provost and a noted New Testament scholar -- he was also a graduate of the United State Naval Academy.

Surely, it must have been the Spirit of God who enlightened me. When a junior officer in the Navy takes his watch in command of a ship, he goes directly to the wheelhouse and takes over the helm. His position signals his role and his authority. In a flash of Spirit-guided insight, I understood the provost's action. When Dr. Mulholland sat in my chair, he was only acting consistently with his understanding and viewpoint on executive command of the Seminary during my absence. The revelation resulted in a chuckle and a wise decision to say nothing about his decision to take the helm of the Seminary from my chair. Knowing Bob as I did, I had the assurance that he would never undercut me, abuse executive power, or try to hang on to the position after my return.

My decision paid off. During the six months of my sabbatical, Dr. Mulholland called me only once to brief me on happenings and I never called him at all. When I returned to the office, I learned that he had to make three critical decisions on policy questions and faculty issues. I cannot forget his debriefing on those decisions after I returned to the office. He said, "I made those decisions without calling you and upsetting your sabbatical because I knew how you would respond to those issues. I tried to do just as you would do." After that conversation, I wanted to send every member of my cabinet to the Naval Academy for a crash course in executive leadership.

My experience at Asbury ran directly counter to a similar situation at Seattle Pacific University. After the Board of Trustees granted me a sabbatical leave after seven years of service, I asked the Vice-president for Institutional Research to serve as chief executive in my absence. He was a gracious and caring person who had excellent relationships with the faculty. More than that, I had full confidence in him because he had served successfully as interim president in his previous position. Two months into the sabbatical, however, I received an emergency phone call from him informing me of a rebellion in the athletic department over a decision that had been made by the new Director of Athletics. Worse yet, the faculty member who had the complaint took his case downtown to be tried in the newspapers, with incendiary results. My interim president was on the verge of panic and I had no choice but to cut short my sabbatical and head home to deal with the issue. After reviewing the volatile situation, I had to dismiss the Director of Athletics and serve notice on the faculty member who made his case a public issue. We survived, but not without undue attention to repairing relationships and re-enforcing policy.

Out of these experiences at Seattle Pacific and Asbury, I framed what I call "The Sabbatical Test." If you are a president and want to assess your executive leadership, take a sabbatical. It will test not just your confidence in your team, but, especially, your confidence in yourself.

THE HIGH TIDE

Early on in my presidential career I adopted the mantra, "Go out on the high tide." From research and experience, I had seen too many successful presidents overstay their welcome. In one setting, for instance, I saw a beloved president rail against a mandatory retirement age of 68 imposed by the board of trustees. Feeling as if he were being persecuted, he let his bitter feelings be known. Soon, however, his bitterness fostered a fatal illness and he died as a relatively young man in his mid-70s. I cite the case because it became a teaching moment in Christian leadership for me.

Institutions move in cycles with rising and falling tides. Presidents also go through cycles of time, energy and attention. The question is whether or not the cycles of institutional need and presidential strengths coincide for the most effective leadership. Presidents can both under-stay and over-stay their welcome. In another example, one of the brightest young leaders was elected to high positions in the church and in higher education. He brought his brilliance to the role by proposing a lofty vision based on sound research and foresight. Once the plan was in place, he moved on to the next leadership role and left behind a befuddled team of administrators trying to implement a vision that was not their own. All of this is to say that timing for the movement of leaders is an all-important, but often neglected, factor in successful leadership. This fact does not contradict the timing for God's call. Instead, it complements the call. The beauty of God's call is the divine match between the gifts of the person and the needs of the institution. On the flipside of the same thought, God's release from the call will be a sense of peace for all concerned.

I press this point in order to say that, in obedience to the call of God, I left on the high tide at all three institutions where I served. This does not mean that the work of presidential leadership was either perfect or perfected. In fact, it means just the opposite. At Spring Arbor College (now University) we left a fully accredited four-year Christian liberal arts college as the fulfilment of my original mandate. At Seattle Pacific University, we left on solid financial grounds with a growing enrollment and exciting potential with university status. At Asbury Theological Seminary, we left one of the best-endowed seminaries for new faculty chairs and capital for such initiatives as the E. Stanley Jones School of World Mission and Evangelism. I made my decision to retire in 1994 because I felt as if the next venture for presidential leadership at Asbury Theological Seminary was a full-orbed fund-raising campaign for student scholarships. Such a campaign would require a minimum of three to four years of demanding presidential time and attention. The schedule could take me into the age of 70, or two years after the Board mandate for retirement at the age of 68. As I reflect again on the decision to leave in 1994, I have a moment of regret. My personal leadership schedule came to its conclusion with plans for the rededication of the campus and its new and remodeled facilities, including the reputation as being the first "smart campus" among theological seminaries. With a twinge of regret, I left that honor to my successor. The fact that a rededication never took place confirms the understanding that every president brings a personal nuance to the role and every past president should close the books on personal expectations.

****

SEEING ALL THINGS WHOLE
THE LOOP IS CLOSED

I NEVER MADE IT to India. But as our son Rob boarded the plane for his flight to Hyderabad, India to teach at Immanuel University and dedicate the McKenna Center for Leadership he said, "Dad, the loop is closed."

Rob's words can never be forgotten. What was the prophetic insight that burst into his consciousness to say that? Through a sleepless night, I was awakened time and time again. The following night I found myself still asking what he meant by "the loop is closed"? The Spirit of God blew open its meaning for me.

This was the first segment for a loop of 60 years with many more segments along the way. Even though I never made a trip to India, I have often said, "If the Lord called me to go to India today, I would be on the first plane out." That commitment gives the loop its continuity through the years and its closure in Rob's words.

PIECES OF THE WHOLE
JANUARY 23, 2015

Rob's ministry in India had the added benefit of his becoming a close friend and brother with Bishop Joab Lohara, founding president of Immanuel University. Earlier, as a model for visionary leadership, Bishop Lohara asked us if he could use our name to raise funds for the Center for Leadership on the Immanuel campus. After we said "Yes" a person-to-person fund drive was successful and the McKenna Center for Leadership was born.

One gift to the Center stands out. Again, Dr. J.C. McPheeters is the key. Columbus, Georgia, home of the Beeson families, is also corporate headquarters for AFLAC, the international insurance firm. During one of his many visits to the Beesons, Dr. McPheeters met the Amos family, founders of AFLAC. He became fast friends with the father, the two sons, and grandson who were to follow him. Paul Amos, one of the sons, specialized in marketing. During one of my visits to Columbus to see the Beesons, I called on Paul, a vibrant Christian leader in his community. Our relationship grew until I invited Paul to be a trustee on the Asbury Board. He accepted and served for a period of time. Then, after one Board meeting, he met with me and said, "Dave, I am not a minister and I don't believe that I have much to bring to the Board." Despite my appeal, he was firm in his decision and resigned his position. Paul soon became president of AFLAC, and with his marketing skills, took the corporation to global dimensions and stature. Later, when we needed marketing expertise for recruiting and fund-raising for the Seminary, I could only think of Paul, with his gifts in marketing which we needed at the Seminary. I live with my regrets. Still, after Paul's death, his son Danny led the way in funding the Paul Amos Chair of Biblical Studies at Asbury. Also, when Danny learned about the Center for Leadership at Immanuel University, he again responded with one of the largest grants to be received, in his parents' name. If we learn from failure, I am the wisest man alive.

TRUSTING FOR CLOSURE
JANUARY 25, 2015

Rob's email to us today told of finding a metallic washer on the road while jogging around the Immanuel campus. He said it was easily visible because it was next to a jagged fracture in the pavement. Then he added, "I am going put the washer on a lanyard and wear it around my neck as a constant reminder of God closing the loop of His good will in a broken world." Later in the day, he brought the symbol of the washer to life when he ministered in a leper colony, praying hands-on with the residents and preaching to the whole community. God is always at work at closing loops and making all things whole. We, however, open up gaps in the loop of His divine purpose by our doubts and fears, sins and stupidities. We also know that the accidents of nature, circumstances out of our control, and the actions of evil forces can cause us to ask if God has forgotten us.

I had a serious gap in the loop of God's will when I answered His call to go back to Asbury Theological Seminary as president. It meant taking Rob from a Christian school where he was just beginning to excel academically to a public school in Kentucky, where fifty percent of the students were their families' first-timers in high school. It meant taking him from stardom on the soccer team to a school that had no soccer. It meant taking him from close friends to start over in a strange land. As we left the freeway around Lexington, Kentucky and entered the narrow roadway into Wilmore, Kentucky, all of my doubts checked in. I looked at Rob in the back seat of the car, felt a stifling crush, and angrily asked God, "What have I done to my son?" A clear voice answered, "Trust Me." Forgive me, Lord. As Rob ministers in India and represents us in the dedication of the McKenna Center for Leadership, I hear a resounding voice saying again, "Trust Me." In the most gracious way God closed the loop to quell my doubts.

LOOP TO LOOP
JANUARY 29, 2015

When pictures of the first Commencement at Immanuel University and Rob's graduation address came through today, the joy of celebration reverberated around the world and into our hearts.

Once again, I thought about a loop and remembered again that in God's grand Gestalt, the whole is greater than the sum of the parts.

Put that thought into the context of closing the loop at Immanuel University today. When I saw Rob, our son, unveiling the plaque, cutting the ribbon, and giving the dedicatory address, I felt closure for the call of God to India 63 years ago. I could say, "It is finished." But then, as I saw the lights, caught the colors, looked into the faces of the people, felt the depth of the hymns, and read Rob's words, the whole truly became so much greater than the sum of the parts. I felt as if the whole place was filled with His glory.

Forgive me, Lord, for assuming that the story is over when we close the loop on our part in doing God's will. This is when we should join Jesus in crying, "*Father, into Your hands I commend my spirit.*" Resurrection awaits us as God Himself draws together the beginning and the end of the loop to seal it with His presence and the promise of His peace. With that confidence we not only say "The loop is closed," but we dare to ask, "What's next, dear Father?"

III

The Call Extended

8

The Church I Love
Our Binding Address

IF YOU TAKE A swab of my heart, the results will show my spiritual DNA. I am a Free Methodist by love, a Wesleyan by choice, and an Evangelical by spirit. Even though my spiritual pedigree may not be blue-blooded according to some theological standards, I am proud to claim my religious ancestry because it is a gift of grace, not an entitlement of heritage. Let me spell out what I mean.

A LOVE STORY

I love the Free Methodist Church. I have already told the story of my introduction to the Free Methodist Church through the Spirit-guided events leading to my enrollment at Spring Arbor Junior College. I count my Spring Arbor years as the crucial time when the threads of grace were woven together into the design for the whole cloth of God's holy will. The rest of the story stretches out over 75 years. Beginning with my college years, I fell in love with the Free Methodist Church, married one of its daughters, received ordination as one of its clergy, and served two of its educational institutions and its affiliated seminary as president. I owe the Free Methodist Church my life and my love.

Memory takes me back to the late 1940s when I was first introduced to Free Methodism.. Signs for local churches carried the name Free Methodist Church along with the designation, *"The Church of the Light and Life Hour,"* a national radio broadcast. As a newcomer, I remember listening to The Light and Life Hour each week and sensing the pride of being a member of the family.

My new love for the church was put to a test when I felt the call to be a Free Methodist pastor. The first step included completion of a course of ministerial study followed by election to probationary status as a prospect for ordination. When my name was presented, vocal opposition came from delegates who knew the reputation of The Evangelistic Mission Tabernacle. Split away from the Free Methodist Church in 1920, the Tabernacle found its identity as a radical offshoot of the parent body. Whereas the Free Methodists prohibited instrumental music in its worship services, the Tabernacle gave free range to piano, brass, strings and percussion accompanying congregational singing. Tabernacle services invited shouts of victory, walking or running through the aisles to the glory of God, and hell-fire sermons attacking sins such as movies, carnivals, drama and any other form of carnal pleasure. Despite the fact that Free Methodists still had a dress code that kept neckties off clergy and cap sleeves off women's dresses, the Tabernacle went one better. Part of every hell-fire sermon was a rant against some violation of the women's dress code or the evil eye of men.

Governance, however, ultimately divided Free Methodists from Tabernacle folk. Free Methodists still followed the authority structure developed by John Wesley—local societies under annual conference jurisdiction and both under the quadrennial meetings of the General Conference (national and global) of the Free Methodist Church. In sharp contrast, Tabernacle governance came into focus in the personal authority of the pastor, whose word was law.

A SENSE OF BELONGING

My sense of belonging in Free Methodist fellowship found major reinforcement on my first visit to Winona Lake, Indiana, headquarters of the Church and gathering place for family reunions at General Conference, youth camps, and missionary meetings. Although the denomination was small, the bonds were strong. Bishops led the way in preaching the Wesleyan doctrine of entire sanctification and calling all members to the unity of faith around our common heritage. All barriers of age, race, gender, education, social status, and geography fell when the family of God gathered for Holy Communion in final services of commitment. Even I, a maverick from the Tabernacle, experienced full acceptance in those moments when the Spirit of God made us one in Christ. I owe a debt of love to the Free Methodist Church.

A GLOBAL REACH

Years later, I chaired the Free Methodist General Conference committee that recommended moving its headquarters from Warsaw to Indianapolis, Indiana in anticipation of a future in global ministry with an international airport close at hand. Critics who rued the loss of family identity and denominational branding were right. We should have included in our recommendation for the move a plan for reinforcing the communal strength of the name and brand of The Free Methodist Church. Despite noble efforts to give the World Missions Center and the Marston Historical Library a centering point for global Free Methodism, we no longer have the same strengths of place and brand that we once knew. Free Methodists, not unlike other evangelical denominations, have forfeited their historic identity for generic names that allegedly give greater acceptance for evangelism in our communities. Admittedly, the name "Free Methodist" has little meaning for a generation that mistrusts all institutions and the authority that they represent. There is nothing wrong in changing the names of local churches to compete with the flurry of independent and megachurch ministries. But something significant is lost when our members lack a sense of belonging to something bigger than the local church.

WHAT'S IN A NAME?

My wife and I had the experience of attending a highly successful church plant that had changed its name from "Free Methodist Church" to a fellowship identified with the local community. Vibrant contemporary worship, neighborly fellowship, and dynamic growth attest to the value of the change. But after we attended for a time, I was asked to serve on the Board of Trustees. In my first meeting, the board chair opened with the humorous introduction, "I attended here for six years before I knew that we had any connection with the Free Methodist Church." We laughed when we should have cried. Certainly, there is merit in belonging to a local and semi-independent fellowship, but we are living in a global community that needs connection with something bigger than our immediate setting and personal interest. The Free Methodist Church is more than a local church or a national church. It is a family of global dimensions, with more than one million members overseas. Much of the overseas growth has come from mergers with other denominations or associations that have accepted our name as well as our governance. Free Methodists in India are our brothers and Free Methodists in Africa are our sisters. Until we have a firm sense of belonging to that global family, we risk becoming victims of a self-contained and self-serving community that belies the Great Commission.

OUR DISTINCTIVE IDENTITY

At the 1994 General Conference, I spoke at a dinner sponsored by the Free Methodist World Conference, under the leadership of Bishop Neandra John from India. My address focused on the "soft side" of our identity as a global family. Recognizing the trend toward independent names among local churches in North America and the adoption of our historic name in global mergers, I proposed a missional paradigm in which:

1. Every nation is a mission field;

2. Every church is a mission station; and

3. Every member is a missionary.

Then, whether or not we accepted the name "Free Methodist" as our individual, local, national or global identifier, I appealed to John Wesley's vision for the unity of personal and social holiness. In place of "The Church of the Light and Life Hour" as the subtitle after our name, I proposed *"Passion for One; Compassion for all."* I can still feel the power of that simple phrase bringing us together around our distinctive claim for personal and social holiness. Sad to say, my idealism was rewarded with informal commendation, but formal inaction.

OUR EDUCATIONAL POTENTIAL

Memory also takes me back to a similar proposal that I made as president of Spring Arbor Junior College to the Association of Free Methodist Educational Institutions (AFMEI) in the early 1960s. Our small denomination of 70,000 members supported seven institutions of Christian higher education (Roberts Wesleyan College, Greenville College, Spring Arbor Junior College, Seattle Pacific College, Wessington Springs College, Central College, and Los Angeles Pacific College). At Spring Arbor Junior College, we were on the cusp of advancing to four-year college status while Roberts Wesleyan College and Greenville College were searching for new presidents. In this time of transition, I foresaw the opportunity for the merger of the three institutions into a Free Methodist University located in Indianapolis, Indiana. After study of the prospects, a proposal was written and presented to the AFMEI and its leadership under Bishop Charles Fairbairn. After bishops of the Church and chairs of the respective boards of trustees reviewed the proposal, a special meeting was called for Chicago, Illinois. Bishop Fairbairn chaired the meeting and announced the conclusion. Looking directly at me, he said, "David, this proposal reminds me of a little boy throwing water through a brick wall." Nothing more need be said. The proposal was dead in the water and I took his conclusion as a mandate to proceed full speed with the plans to make Spring Arbor a four-year Christian liberal arts college.

A DREAM DEFERRED

Twice, then, my dreams for my Church have been frustrated. Today, you can go online for the websites of our most successful churches and sometimes find no Free Methodist identifier at all unless it is buried in fine print. Five of our seven schools still exist, some under title of "University," and the merger of Los Angeles Pacific College with Azusa Bible College has resulted in Azusa Pacific University, an affiliate member of the AFMEI. Ironically, I served as consultant for the merger.

Today, the relationship of the colleges and universities to the parent Church is a test, not just for significance, but for survival. Multiple factors, led by the LBGTQ movement and Critical Race Theory with their legal implications, are causing deep divisions within our institutions and creating a crisis of enrollment and economics never seen before. As if these challenges were not enough, the nature of the relationship between the schools and the parent body is even more critical. In 1960 a study for the merger of the Free Methodist Church with the Wesleyan Church was completed. Theologically, the merger seemed like a match made in heaven, but two organizational factors stood in the way. One was the title of leadership. Free Methodists had their bishops and the Wesleyans had their general superintendent. The other was the question of church-college relationships. Free Methodist schools were affiliated with the Church, but not owned by the Church. In sharp contrast, Wesleyan schools were owned by the Church and subject to final decisions by the parent body. The merger fell apart because neither institution was willing to change its authority for leadership or its legal connection with its colleges. For Free Methodist schools today, the long-standing affiliation by mission and theology without ownership is coming to contest at every level of legal and educational relationships. The future is tenuous without some legal, financial, and spiritual breakthroughs that will define and redefine the nature of the Free Methodist college and university. The image of the little boy trying to throw water through a brick wall comes back to haunt me.

OUR SPIRITUAL POTENTIAL

In 1996, I authored an updated history of the Free Methodist Church under the title, *A Future with a History*. Statistics tell their own story. In 1960, the base year for the history, Free Methodist churches in North America totaled 70,000 members. To foster growth our Board of Bishops proposed "Double in a Decade." Their strategy was evangelism for the unreached through the local church and personal evangelism. Although I gave full support to the initiative, my curiosity prompted me to ask, "The emphasis is on out-reach. What about our in-reach?"

The question led me to do a study on the holding power of our local churches for the children of our families. Astounding results came to light. If we were able to hold just one quarter of the young people who dropped out of the Free Methodist Church sometime in their teens, we would double in a decade! Yet, out-reach won out and when I wrote the history in 1996, our national membership still totaled approximately 70,000. At the time of this writing, 27 years later, total adult membership in the United States is 62,000 members or 4.3 percent of the global membership of the Free Methodist Church.

In *A Future with a History*, I traced some of the strategic initiatives that had been proposed for the Church over the last half of the 20th century. Beginning with personal evangelism, revival meetings and crusade ministries, the proposals stretched out to church growth and church planting initiatives. Currently, proposals for leadership development are leading the way.

While it is worthwhile to assess the progress of the Church toward these goals over the past half-century, the prior question should be, "To what extent are these strategies contributing to seeing the vision, stating the mission, and setting the tone of the Church?" More specifically, "To what extent have they been effective in renewing the Church in changing times?" "Most important of all, "What should be our priority for the future?" Permit me to return to the final words of *A Future with a History*. From the perspective of age and the evidence of experience, I write again:

> In the lofty dreams of the old, we see our past; in the faithful ministry of today's sons and daughters, we see our present; and in the visions of the young, we see our future. With confidence in this promise, the Free Methodist Church has a future in its history.[1]

With this towering truth in mind, I ask the privilege of a final appeal for the Church I love.

****

SEEING ALL THINGS WHOLE
OUR BINDING ADDRESS

Without a "binding address," nothing can be whole. A binding address is defined as the core identity of an institution, whether religious or secular. Most often, the core identity has a singular focus that embraces all other aspects of institutional meaning and motivation. John Wesley, our founder, leads the way with his thought-provoking and energizing statement, "*I look upon all the world as my parish.*"[2] Within a short sentence of five words we see a vision for redemption of the whole world spelled out in the ministry of the local parish. Under the power of these five words, Wesley led an evangelical revival for England that saved the

1. McKenna, *A Future With a History*, 332.
2. Wesley, *Journal*, June 11, 1739.

nation from a revolution that devastated France in the same era. A "binding address" with a holistic vision is our priority need for the church today. Here are the outworkings of my plea.

OUR DISTINCT IDENTITY

First, *I plead for an identity of Free Methodism that sees our vision, defines our mission and sets the tone for personal and social holiness in the Wesleyan context.*

Remember again, Colossians 1:1, *"He is before all thing and in Him all things hold together."* What holds our Church together? In the 28 years since I wrote *A Future with a History*, individualism has made deep inroads into the clarity of a holiness church and into the strength of our established institutions. When I speak of holiness, I am referring directly to the question of our identity. "Do we know who are and why we are here?" The distinctive of our faith is the doctrine of biblical holiness or entire sanctification fleshed out in the experience and practice of wholeness.

When Wesley Duewel surveyed holiness constituencies several years ago, he found that few members of our churches understood the doctrine and even fewer professed the experience. His study needs to be repeated today. "How many of our members understand the doctrine and how many claim the experience?" As current surveys of Evangelical Christians show yawning gaps between profession and practice, we can make an educated guess that the Wesleyan doctrine of holiness is still misunderstood and neglected. Somehow, some way, our distinctive biblical and Wesleyan identity (call it "branding" if you wish) needs to be clearly spoken and graphically symbolized as a guide, not just for our Church, but for every member. As a starter thought for our "binding address," I again suggest *"Passion for One; Compassion for All."*

OUR MISSIONAL UNITY

Next, I plead for the unity of our primary institutions in the mission of the Church.

Francis Asbury rode 260,000 miles back and forth across the Appalachian Mountains under the Spirit-guided impulse declared by John Wesley as his understanding of Methodism's purpose: "*To reform the nation and, in particular, the Church, to spread scriptural holiness over the land.*" Free Methodist pioneers shared a similar vision for their trek across America. As the movement marched West, our pioneers followed a familiar sequence—building their homes, churches, schools, orphanages, medical facilities, and retirement centers. You can trace the trek of Free Methodists across the country in the founding of their colleges— Roberts Wesleyan, Greenville, Spring Arbor, Wessington Springs, Central, Los Angeles Pacific, and Seattle Pacific. From the standpoint of size and resources, the establishment of this number of schools is absurd. But from the unified vision of home, church, and school for the nurture of the young and the maturity of its members, these institutions are integral to our witness.

OUR EDUCATIONAL POTENTIAL

My mind now races *to a compelling vision for a future of Free Methodist higher education.* A poignant example leaped out at me while reading the history of the Evangelical movement in the United States. The story is heavily weighted toward Reform dominance, while Wesleyans are treated like theological and intellectual tagalongs. In 1971, however, when the Christian College Consortium was organized, seven of the twelve members were identified with the Wesleyan holiness tradition and three of the seven were Free Methodist colleges! The author skipped over this fact but noted that the twelve members represented elite schools in Christian higher education. As a former Free Methodist college president, I confess my bias, but not without appealing for today's Church to renew its relationship with these institutions and claim them as its own. The same appeal can be made for other educational institutions and social agencies across the globe that carry the name "Free Methodist" high on their masthead.

Throughout my career, I was enriched by participation with other college presidents in the Association of Free Methodist Educational Institutions (AFMEI). After our retirement, we were witness to the expansion of Free Methodism across the globe and the establishment of other institutions of higher education, such as Hope Africa University, Immanuel University, and Haiti International University. In a moment of inspiration, I exercised my emeritus rights and proposed that the AFMEI become the Association of Free Methodist Education International with our global partners as full members. Imagine the potential for such partnership. Networking, online courses, faculty and student exchanges are only the beginning. Higher education may well be the best avenue for transforming Free Methodism into a truly global Church.

OUR PRIMARY TASK

Finally, *I plead for the Free Methodist Church to adopt the Wesleyan model of holiness as the means for discipling our converts and maturing our members.* Our mind goes immediately to the organizations, bands, and class meetings that give the Wesleyan movement its unique character. Societies were large group gatherings, i.e. worship, for biblical teaching and learning. Classes were smaller, diverse groups that welcomed inquiring seekers and aimed at changing behavior. Bands were smaller, homogeneous groups where soul-searching or "close conversation" led to changing motives and affections. Penitent bands were again small groups of persons who repented of sins and sought recovery from the consequences of sin. So, from inquiring seekers to penitent sinners, the system provided a personalized sense of care and communion. Without a doubt, the holistic Wesleyan model for maturing its members is a Spirit-guided stroke of genius.

While in full support of the Wesleyan system of societies, classes, and bands, our homes still lead the way. God gave Moses the best definition of holiness as a personal experience when He said, *"Love the Lord with all your heart, soul, mind and strength."* *(Deut. 6:5).* Immediately, then, God made personal holiness a family experience:

> *"These commandments that I give you today are to be upon your hearts. Impress them upon your children. Talk about them when you sit at home and when you walk along the road, when you lie down and when you sit up. Tie them as symbols on your hands and bind them on your foreheads. Write them upon the doorframes of your homes and on your gates."*
> (Deut.6:6–9)

Symbols, teaching, and modeling of the Spirit-filled life should make the Free Methodist Church known as "the Family Church." From dedication or baptism at birth there should be a line of development through the equals of catechism, baptism, and confirmation and into the Wesleyan model of classes for developing spiritual maturity and lay or ordained denominational leadership. Belonging to the Body of Christ, then, is our highest level of priority. Whether the programs that bring us together are legal, financial, educational, or spiritual, the common cause is personal and social holiness. From small groups that model the original class meeting to global missions that make us one with all people, a sense of belonging may well be our holding power against the forces of self-interest that threaten to split us apart and leave us lonely and lost.

A MOMENT OF REGRET

In the 1970s, a scholarship fund under the name "Free Methodist Futures" was proposed and adopted by the Board of Administration. Students from Free Methodist churches attending Free Methodist colleges were given a grant of $300 toward tuition costs. The purpose was not just to encourage Free Methodist students to attend Free Methodist colleges, but to build the relationship of youth to the church both in college and after. The program had a good start but a short life. With the first budget crunch. Free Methodist Futures was among the first to go, easily forgotten and never restored. Dare I propose that a strategic initiative such as Free Methodist Futures may well be the open secret to building and maintaining the mother Church? Statistics show that a wide variety of evangelistic thrusts have failed us over the past 70 or more years since "Double in a Decade" was proposed. Why not shift the priority of the Church to the inward reach of our children and families? Imagine a denominational priority for raising an endowment large enough to fund scholarships at Free Methodist colleges and universities for Free Methodist youth. Both our churches and our schools are under fire from the salvos of secularism that have already taken a toll on our distinctive identity, mission, and ministry. Every signal in our society points to a future in which survival for our churches and schools will be at stake. Our hope is in our youth, and we have the resources of strong and viable Christian colleges and universities, not just to serve them, but to serve the Church as well. We need Free Methodist Futures in our future.

A FAMILY OF FAITH

When the questions of "Who?" we are and "Why?" rise to salience among Free Methodists, we have to bow before the truth that we are called to be a family of faith with the strength of belonging that reaches out to serve sacrificially the lonely and the lost. Out of our Wesleyan heritage, this is the integration of personal and social holiness at its best.

The core questions of "Who?" and "Why?" we are as Free Methodists must be answered with clarity for persons in the pews. Continuing attempts to lead with the strategy of "What?" and the tactics of "How?" will leave us chasing after the latest technique borrowed from the secular culture. In response to the loneliness caused by the extremes of individualism in our day, the Free Methodist Church still has the mind and the heart to offer a special sense of belonging in the family of God. Our prayer is for the wholeness

of heart, mind, and spirit that gave impetus to the founding of the
Free Methodist Church and still holds its promise for the future.

9

The Faith I Embrace
The Great Synthesis

I AM A WESLEYAN by choice. Yet, the first sermon I heard on
the text, *"...be holy because I am holy"* (Leviticus 11:14) almost destroyed my faith. Earlier, in *The Triumphs of His Grace: A Spiritual
Odyssey*, I told my story of a holiness camp-meeting when I was
first introduced to the Wesleyan doctrine of entire sanctification.
Under the guise of Biblical truth, the message of entire sanctification came to me in three tightly-tied packages. To be holy as
God is holy meant: sinless perfection; (2) carnal extraction; and (3)
groveling humility. As a result, I carried into adulthood the nag-
ging sense of guilt along with the lack of assurance for my salvation. Somehow, I knew that this view of holiness did not coincide
with the view of Jesus the Christ, Paul the Apostle, or John the
Wesleyan.

A BLIP ON THE SCREEN

My search for holiness and wholeness hit another snag during my seminary years. As a first-year student, I discovered the
field of pastoral psychology. The spark of interest took me to the

University of Michigan hospital for a summer course in the field as a chaplain intern under the Institute for Pastoral Care. Before I left for Ann Arbor, my Seminary professors warned me that the field of psychology was an enemy of our faith.

When I returned to Seminary in the fall, I wrote a paper for a course in Romans under the title, "The Neurosis of the Law." During the summer, I had been introduced to Karen Horney's theory of neurosis. In her classic study, *Neurosis and Human Growth: The Struggle for Self-Realization* she posited that neurosis is the disparity between the "Ideal Self" and the "Real Self." Neurotics create expectations for themselves that they can never reach, and when they fail, they only reach higher again. In her chapter on "The Tyranny of the Should," she describes neurosis as being torn between their expectations for perfection and their self-hate for failure.[1] For the paper I wrote, I read Horney's theory into Paul's confession in Romans 7:21–24 when he wrote,

> *"When I want to do good, evil is right there with me. For in my inner being I delight in God's law, but I see another law at work in the members of the body, waging war against the law of my mind and making me a prisoner of the law of sin at work within my members. What a wretched man I am! Who will rescue me from this body of death?"*

I made two mistakes in my interpretation. For one, I used psychology to interpret Scripture. For the other, I presumed that Paul was speaking about the continuing struggle that he experienced after, as well as before, his sanctification. My approach ignited a theological fire of major proportions. The professor to whom I submitted the paper called me into his office and sternly pronounced "Anathema" on my thesis. In no uncertain terms, he let me know that human psychology can never be used to interpret Scripture. Furthermore, Paul's confession of the conflict comes to conclusion when he writes,

> *"Therefore, there is now no condemnation for those who are in Christ Jesus,*

1. Horney, *Neurosis and Human Growth.*

*because through Christ Jesus the law of the Spirit of life set
me from free from the law of sin and death."* (Romans 8:
1–2).

My professor interpreted this text to say that all conflict between self and Christ comes to rest when we are instantaneously
sanctified by His Holy Spirit. I was thrown back upon a more sophisticated version of eradication theory or "de-kittenizing" the
well. No room was left for those of us who still struggle with self in
the process of "becoming" sanctified as well as "being" sanctified.

As an outcome of this professor-student conference, I was
denied my scholarship from the Free Methodist Church because I
aspired to graduate study in pastoral psychology rather than going
directly to the local parish. With a little bit of humorous self-satis-
faction, I never mentioned this fact after I became president of the
Seminary. The biggest tickle, however, came when the professor
who scorched me for interpreting Scripture through psychology
asked me to perform his marriage to the Seminary librarian. Holiness is not without humor.

SABBATICAL INSIGHTS

Cycling back to the scholarship I lost, you can imagine the fun
when my reputation as a Wesleyan synthesizer took me back to
the presidency of Asbury Theological Seminary. In preparation
for that role, Seattle Pacific University provided a six-week sabbatical in the final months of my presidency to study as a visiting
scholar in the Wesley library at Cambridge University in England.
Day after day, I poured through Wesley's sermons and Wesleyan
history in order to cast a vision for leadership at Asbury. The cul-
mination of my study came in an address that I presented to the
North American section of the World Methodist Council. Under
the title of "What a Time to Be a Wesleyan," I summed up what I
had discovered in three statements that reflect the genius of the
Wesleyan message for integrating opposites of truth:

1. If You Can't Think It, Don't Believe It—a plea for uniting reason and revelation in our Wesleyan faith;

2. If You Can't Sing it, Don't Preach It—a plea for balancing truth and grace in our Wesleyan worship, and

3. If You Can't Live it, Don't Push it—a plea for connecting personal and social holiness in our Wesleyan witness.

These three statements followed me through my time as president of Asbury. Along with them, I proposed *"World Wesleyan Leadership"* as the mantra for our time at the Seminary. At our inauguration in 1983, we scored a first by telecasting the keynote address by Charles Colson and the inaugural ceremony itself for our alumni and friends via satellite to sites across North America. Twelve years later, at the time of my retirement, we celebrated *World Wesleyan Leadership"* by hosting the North American section of the World Methodist Council on campus with satellite transmission to Leeds, England for an address and discussion with Donald English, President of the World Methodist Council. The stage was set. Asbury became known as the first "smart campus" in theological education.

Asbury is an independent seminary in the Wesleyan theological tradition. Free Methodists are closely connected through the John Wesley Seminary Foundation that maintains a presence on campus and funds scholarship aid for Free Methodist students attending Asbury. I was the first non-United Methodist president at Asbury. Suspicions about my theological ancestry surfaced in the discussion among members of the Board of Trustees prior to my election. One prominent member and major financial contributor resigned from the Board after my election. The issue never surfaced again.

When I represented both Asbury Seminary and the Free Methodist Church at meetings of the World Methodist Council, I felt the arms of belonging extended to global dimensions. I also learned that God had a special role for me as a member, and later an officer, of the North American Section of the WMC. Methodist denominations have the rich heritage of holiness, but sometimes forget their birth. On more than one occasion, it was my lot to remind the world body of our distinction as advocates of entire sanctification and as agents of John Wesley's call to wholeness.

FROM WILMORE TO THE WORLD

In 1987, I gave the keynote address for the World Methodist Council in Nairobi, Kenya on the conference theme, "Jesus Christ, Only Hope for Our Salvation." (19) To stand on that platform at Nairobi and speak to Wesleyans from around the world is a far stretch from the Appalachian village of Wilmore, Kentucky where Asbury is located, and even farther from the holiness Tabernacle in Ypsilanti, Michigan. A few days after my keynote, the secretary of the World Council of Churches addressed the same assembly. His speech directly countered mine. Taking the ecumenical spirit to its extreme, he preached that we had to reduce the sharp edges of our faith in order to be part of an emerging order of world religions. His message was loud and clear, "Jesus Christ, NOT the Only Hope for Our Salvation." When the media spotted the difference between our speeches, they invited us to a press conference. Strange spot for a Tabernacle kid, defending Jesus Christ as the "exclusive" source for our salvation against a world religious leader for whom "inclusion" was the highest truth.

REVIVING PERSONAL AND SOCIAL HOLINESS

Reflecting back upon the rich experiences that I had as a member of the World Methodist Council and as a vice-president for the North American section, two theological fault lines were exposed. One was *the loss of emphasis for the definitive experience of personal holiness*. Perfection may have been a theological fault of an earlier time, but dilution is no better. Wesleyans of all stripes need to be constantly reminded of the truth that justifies their existence.

The second fault comes to light in *the desire to make the faith relevant in the contemporary mind*. With the delicate balance between personal holiness and social holiness, the push for relevance often tips the scale toward social holiness and the heresy of Pelagianism, the tendency to substitute works for faith. The secretary of the World Council of Churches took that position when he advocated a softening of the Wesleyan position on the nature of God in order to cooperate with other gods. Even more specifically, one of the key issues for debate at the Nairobi conference was whether or not Wesleyan theology was compatible with Liberation Theology and its Marxist connections. The natural desire to be relevant lurks as a danger for every generation of Wesleyans.

****

SEEING ALL THINGS WHOLE
THE GREAT SYNTHESIS

I cannot escape my Wesleyan heritage. When David Hubbard introduced me as "The Great Synthesizer" he paid me the compliment of being a person who works to see all things whole. Later, I found out that I was in good company. John Wesley was criticized for failing to have a systematic theology as well-defined as John Calvin's Institutes. He opted for a practical theology revealed through his preaching. In other words, John Wesley is the one who qualifies as "The Great Synthesizer" when he identifies our holiness as well as our wholeness in the work of the Spirit who:

- *enlightens our understanding,*
- *rectifies our will and affections,*
- *renews our nature,*
- *unites us with Christ,*
- *assures our adoption as God's children,*
- *guides our action,*
- *purifies and sanctifies our souls and bodies;*

- *for the purpose of "full and eternal enjoyment of God*[2]

John Wesley fused the truth of revelation together with the grace of daily living and found the fuel for empowering one of greatest spiritual awakenings in Christian history.

OUR WORLD PARISH

We who are Wesleyans inherit the vision of John Wesley when he said, "*I look upon all of the world as my parish.*" In these oft-quoted words we see the meaning of wholeness. A scope that embraces "all of the world" might be viewed as a figment of Wesley's imagination except for the fact that he anchors his vision in the commitment to "my parish." In other words, he is both a global visionary and a parish priest. When bonded and functioning together, they give us our model for ministry as Wesleyans. We are called to see our world and to serve our world. Once again, God's grand design puts the pieces together into a tapestry of grace and the whole becomes greater than the sum of the parts.

Make room for a Wesleyan synthesizer. In the delicate Wesleyan balance between personal and social holiness, I am witness to the demand for social relevance that dogs the steps of every religious movement. Social holiness is a legitimate demand upon our loyalty, but not at the expense of a fractured faith. We cannot give away personal holiness for social holiness. Nor can we neglect social holiness by an imbalance on personal holiness. Relevance is not the answer to our brokenness.

OUR GLOBAL GUIDE

Nathan Hatch, in his celebrated book, *The Democratization of America*, shows us the model for wholeness in personal and social holiness.[3] With a stroke of Spirit-guided genius, Methodist circuit-riders moved West across pioneer territory under the mandate,

2. Bevins, "Pneumatology," 102.

3. Hatch, *Democratization of American Christianity*, 1989.

"To spread scriptural holiness across the land and reform the nation." Hatch reasons that this motivation actually saved the nation from a split between East and West that might have resulted in a civil war not unlike the later conflict between North and South. It took a mission statement with precision and accountability for Francis Asbury to ride 260,000 miles on horseback back and forth across the Appalachian Mountains. The same sense of mission motivated hundreds of circuit-riders and pioneer pastors to join in the venture. One can only ask whether the mission statements that we read on the website and in the publications of Wesleyan Holiness churches today carry the same incentive for commitment and sacrifice.

OUR CONSUMING PASSION

My Wesleyan passion continues to be putting broken things together and making them holy and whole. Our historical incentive is to demonstrate again how personal holiness and social holiness are inseparable. This is no small task in a world that is as badly broken as ours and among persons who are as badly broken as we are. Such a task runs counter to every impulse in our fast-moving and deeply conflicted world. We are not only broken-up, but we are burned-out from our unbalanced efforts to make sense out of the pieces and find meaning in the puzzle. As never before, we need Wesleyan theology to put the pieces together and Wesleyan practice to show us the whole picture.

10

The Witness I Share
A Prophetic Minority

I AM AN EVANGELICAL because my spirit resonates with the biblical meaning of the name. "Evangelical" is the root word for the Good News of the Gospel. I was introduced to the Evangelical movement in the mid-1950s at the age of 25, after seminary graduation, and in my first administrative position in Christian higher education. My earlier spiritual journey had taken me from the most rigid of religious restrictions to the relative freedom of Wesleyan doctrine and practice. To learn that "Evangelical" meant the affirmation and communication of "Good News" was all I needed. I registered for my first National Association of Evangelicals convention in Chicago, Illinois. Awe-struck by the names Billy Graham, Harold Ockenga, Carl F. H. Henry, and Leslie Marston, I quickly learned the history of the struggle to free biblically-based Christianity from grace-choking Fundamentalism to the Good News of Evangelicalism. Membership in NAE meant belief in the: (1) personal conversion through rebirth in Jesus Christ; (2) full inspiration and authority of the Word of God; (3) atonement through the cross, death, and resurrection of Jesus Christ; and (4) sharing the Good

News of the Gospel through public witness and social action. The history of the movement comes in three dramas:

A PASSIVE MAJORITY
1950-1970

American Evangelicals found their footing during the post-WW II period of the 1950s. It is best described as a time when American minds were as "quiet as mice." Public confidence rode high behind the presidency of Dwight Eisenhower, the prospects for economic boom, the idealism of educational opportunity, the dream of a moon-shot, and the triumph of democracy undergirded by the Judeo-Christian faith. According to Eisenhower, a Military-Industrial- Academic complex set the pace for progress in Reconstruction. Militarily, we had the strength of the world's leading superpower to preserve the peace; industrially, we had the incentive and know-how to restore a prosperous economy; and academically, we had the brain power to lead and guide toward a humanistic vision of "*life, liberty and the pursuit of happiness.*" Religion, particularly in the Protestant tradition, found new confidence in liberal theology and the social gospel. The Council of Churches led the way behind its assumption that the new millennium would be known by the title of its informal house organ, "*The Christian Century.*"

Economic justice, civil rights, and religious ecumenism stood high on the agenda of liberal Christians. Neither they nor we, conservative believers, heard the rumblings of revolution that would undermine the allegedly stable moral climate of the 1950s. At that time: (1) abortion was a crime; (2) same-sex marriage was illegal; (3) homosexuality qualified as a psychiatric deviation; and (4) divorce occurred in a minority of marriages. Everything was in place for a spiritual revival or a social revolution.

Not that all was rosy in the 1950s. The ugly head of prejudice, hatred, and vengeance reared up in the likes of Senator Joe McCarthy and his anti-Communism campaign. Every tactic of vindication came into play in the Congressional hearings and Justice Department actions against a vaguely defined enemy of democracy. As with other hate campaigns, McCarthy and company were ultimately discredited, but not before the national trust was damaged and evil intent went underground to wait another day.

While Evangelical Christianity was born in a national climate of relative stability, a civil war was tearing apart conservative Christian faith. Fundamentalists, led by Carl McIntyre, demanded lock-step obedience to inerrancy, separatism and dispensationalism. Enemies were defined, not just in opposition to the social gospel of the National Council of Churches, but also against Billy Graham's policy of collaboration with mainline churches in his crusades. Fundamentalism lost. Behind the rising public influence of Billy Graham, the theological reputation of Harold Ockenga, and the academic credentials of Carl F. H. Henry, the National Association of Evangelicals was born as the voice for the "Good News" of the Gospel.

As a young Christian idealist, my introduction to the Evangelical spirit came with the reading of Carl F. H. Henry's landmark book *The Uneasy Conscience of Modern Fundamentalism*.[1] Although Carl was a classic Calvinist steeped in Reform theology, he foresaw the need for a social witness to balance the theological witness of Evangelicals. Weighing the options of his four "R's" for social witness—Redemption, Reform, Resistance and Revolution—I opted for the reform process of education, legislation, and social service as the extension of my Christian witness. Would the NAE be the vehicle for the exercise of my passion?

At the annual convention of the National Association of Evangelicals in 1959, I was invited to give the keynote address. Nationally, we were on the verge of a "Jesus Movement" that attracted young and often radical activists to the faith. Hoping that the conservative denominations in the NAE shared the vision of spiritual awakening, I spoke on the subject, "Are Jesus's Kids Joel's Children?" My purpose was obvious from the title. I asked whether or not we were on the cusp of spiritual awakening through the off-beat evidence of God at work among the unlikely. Only one

1. Henry, *Uneasy Conscience*, 1947.

response to my speech is remembered. Hudson Armerding, President of Wheaton College and a respected mentor, took me aside to say, "Dave, we are not yet ready for this."

A FRACTURED IDEALISM

His words took a big bite out of my idealism. I had hoped that NAE would be the vehicle for expressing two of my dreams. One, I hoped that the Association would take the lead in the witness of social holiness, the complement to personal holiness in my Wesleyan ancestry. Two, I foresaw NAE as a prelude to a cooperative arrangement among Evangelical Christian colleges that would multiply their potential for impact in the academic community. In both cases, my hopes were frustrated by the reality that denominational differences drive new initiatives toward the lowest common denominator.

At the same time, I have to recognize that the major Evangelical thrust of the movement came outside the organizational limits of NAE. Under the visionary impact of Billy Graham, crusade rallies took hold across the nation, and most important of all, his initiative in the print media for *Christianity Today* was nothing less than a stroke of Spirit-guided genius. Evangelicalism, despite its limits, was posed for penetrating the culture.

A CONFLICTED HEGEMONY
1960–1976

When the 1950s turned into the 1960s, we can honestly say "All hell broke loose." While Evangelicals fidgeted on the sidelines, our society went through the throes of a social and moral revolution. Assassinations of Jack Kennedy, Martin Luther King, Jr., and Bobby Kennedy give historical accent to the upheaval. Violence on the bridge at Selma, hatred in the rise of Weathermen, degradation in mud at Woodstock, doubt about the Vietnam war, and unchecked protests at the Democratic National Convention in Chicago all tried to put out the light of the "City on a hill." They failed, but not without changing the alleged innocence of the past for the radical intentions of the future.

If the 1960s had a turning point, the conflict over civil rights qualifies. At personal and political risk, Lyndon Baines Johnson made civil and voting rights for our Black citizens the centerpiece of his "Great Society" policy. Sadly, this universal issue fell victim to party politics. Even though Johnson pressured Congress to pass the Civil Rights Act of 1965 and the Voting Rights Acts of 1966, most Evangelicals either dragged their feet or held their tongues.

A BLAND RESPONSE

How did Evangelicals respond to the cataclysms of the 1960s? In the mid-60s, I chaired the Social Action Committee of the NAE. As a standing committee, our charge was to bring resolutions for social action to the plenary body for debate and decision. In light of happenings across the country, we never lacked for issues out of which to frame resolutions. But, almost without exception, the resolutions that we brought to the floor fell victim to the influence of the lowest common denominator. With an eye toward their constituencies, leaders of 50 different denominations would not take the risk of controversy. Bland resolutions became the standard fare for the Evangelical response to revolutionary times.

A POLITICAL TAKEOVER

Perhaps as prognostication of things to come, I recall my introduction to the President's Prayer Breakfast in the mid-1960s. Because the prayer breakfast movement began in Seattle under the leadership of Abraham Vereide, I felt special affinity with its spirit and its potential for Evangelical penetration of the prevailing culture, especially in the Deep State of Washington politics. I was in for disappointment. After preliminaries that emphasized prayer as our national asset, President Lyndon Baines Johnson gave the address. Without apology, he used the platform to justify his use of fire-bombing villages in the Vietnamese conflict. As shocked as I was by this distortion of the purpose of the prayer breakfast, I was more shocked when Billy Graham gave a response justifying the position that President Johnson had taken by quoting, "*I came not bring peace, but a sword.*" *(Matt. 10:34)* Later, Billy would repent of his words, but in this moment the damage was done. Collusion between secular and spiritual powers was evident. On the way back to my hotel after the breakfast, two newscasters shared the cab with me. Even though they were not Christians, they expressed dismay at the loss of integrity for the purpose of the prayer breakfast. This was just the beginning.

A POPULAR PLURALITY
1976–1990

Satan has many weapons in his arsenal of deception. One of the most effective is an attack on the unguarded flank of his enemy. This is what happened in the 1970s with the Evangelical movement. While preparing for a frontal attack on the faith, Satan caught us off guard by vaulting Evangelicals to the front edge of national consciousness. Against the dark background of Kent State killings, Vietnam massacres, and Richard Nixon's treason, the unbelievable happened. According to the media, America was in the midst of a "Born Again" movement when countless numbers were confessing Christ and professing to be Evangelical. *Time* magazine topped off the media wave by naming 1976 as "The Year of the Evangelical." The numbers were astounding. As many as 50 million Americans counted themselves as Evangelical based on the experience of being "born again." Was this unexpected recognition another attack of the enemy on our unguarded flank? Only time would tell.

A MORAL CONTRADICTION

On this high tide, Jerry Falwell appeared with his political claim for a "Moral Majority" comprised primarily of Evangelical Christians, but with open arms to anyone who embraced his pro-life, pro-family, pro-defense, and pro-Israel agenda. Jerry and I became friends when we served together on consultations among Evangelical leaders. How well I recall trying to engage him in conversation about common concerns of our faith position. Nothing caught fire until I mentioned my love for football. Jerry leaned over the table, looked me in the eye and said "Dave, the time is coming when my Liberty University will play Notre Dame in our own stadium."

"Ah, ha," I thought. I found the real heartbeat of the man. (Note: If you watch big-time college football today, you know that he was not far from wrong.)

At the same time, Jerry made it clear that my Wesleyan theology was out-of-bounds for his Fundamentalist theological tenets. I knew to whom he referred when he said that speakers in chapel at his Liberty University had to prescribe to the tenets of his position. Not even Billy Graham qualified as a speaker because he cooperated with liberal Christians in his crusades. Yet, in the same breath, Falwell welcomed non-believers to the Moral Majority who supported his agenda.

A few years later, I personally learned what it means when a politicized agenda ousts Christians and welcomes non-believers. Francis and Edith Shaeffer, accompanied by Everett Koop, Surgeon General of the United States, and Dr. Mildred Jefferson, a prominent surgeon and pro-life advocate from Massachusetts General Hospital, led a national tour under the title, "Whatever Happened to the Human Race?"[2] When the tour stopped at Seattle, my wife and I hosted the principals for dinner at the top of the Space Needle. All went well until Edith Schaffer asked Dr. Jefferson about her faith. Responding quickly and frankly, the doctor said, "I gave up my Christian faith years ago." Shock waves rocked the table. The Schaffers had assumed that because Dr. Jefferson spoke with

---

2. Schaeffer and Koop, *Whatever Happened to the Human Race?*, 1979.

a national voice for the pro-life position, she had to be Christian. Then and there, I foresaw how Satan can use moral issues to divide Christians or lump them into a political cohort under the label of "Evangelicals."

POWER TO TRUTH

For me, the pivotal moment came in 1983 when Ronald Reagan became the first United States president to accept the invitation to address an NAE annual convention. He chose that moment to condemn the USSR as the "Evil Empire." The overwhelming and standing applause of his Evangelical audience still rings in my ears. The die was cast. Unwittingly, NAE had been drawn into partnership with the Reagan presidency and the offshoots of Conservative Republicanism, Christian Nationalism, and The Moral Majority At least in the public eye, all "born-again" believers were lumped into the cohort of "Evangelicals" for political purposes.

A CO-OPTED CONVENTION

One of the stepping-stones to the NAE Presidency was to plan and chair the national convention. My turn came in 1976 at the annual convention in Minneapolis, Minnesota. When I presented some of my initial thoughts about the theme for the program and the speakers who might be engaged, I hit a roadblock when I proposed Senator Mark Hatfield for the keynote address. In no uncertain terms I learned why some church leaders accused NAE of being captive of conservative, right-wing politics. No one had the slightest question about the Senator's faith and witness, but his pacifist position on the buildup of nuclear arms put him outside the tacit position of NAE in favor of a strong national defense, including nuclear arms.

A prolonged debate among the executive committee members of the NAE aired all sides of the question. I, for one, felt as if the Association must avoid the charge of leaning toward right-wing,

Christian nationalism. Even though some of the church leaders feared that their constituencies might not agree with the decision to put Senator Hatfield in the keynote position, I held firm and they graciously agreed to let the invitation be sent. Of course, when I told the Senator about the episode he laughed and said that he was considered an Evangelical with an asterisk—a choice servant of God with a qualification.

As might be expected, Senator Hatfield's keynote rang true on every note and its spirit reverberated through the conference halls. With the wisdom of the Spirit, he framed his position on national defense through the nuclear buildup within the larger context of a call to personal integrity and consistency for every church and every member. A standing ovation sealed the moment and opened the door for NAE members to engage in vigorous conversation about the movement and its independence from political captivity.

WHAT'S IN A NAME?

Evangelicals are now captives in a grab-bag of conservative politics created by the news media and aided by our own lack of clarity. The natural response is to find a new name that will sort out bearers of the Good News from those who use their faith to justify their politics. Any change will be painful, but our identity as a Good News movement will suffer most. Already, Evangelicals are being labeled as "Christian Nationalists" and "White Supremacists" – peevish and paranoid, especially on politically-correct issues related to sexual preferences, sexual relationships, and sexual behavior. Under the guise of equality in these matters, Robert Bellah's "Utilitarian self-interest" rears its ugly head and defined as "doing what we want to do for our own profit." To compound the issue, Utilitarian self-interest is joined by what Bellah calls "Express self-interest" or "being what we want to be for our own pleasure."[3]

In this climate, Evangelicals are learning the meaning of the adage, "When you are in control, we demand our rights; when we

3. Bellah, *Habits of the Heart*, 41ff.

are in control, you have no rights." The demand for equality goes back as far as the Garden of Eden when Satan promised Adam and Eve in the garden that if they ate the fruit of the tree of life, they would *"...be like God, knowing good and evil."* (Gen. 3:5) The results are going to be the same. Original sin will once again be in control.

What is our option as Evangelicals? Even though critics will charge my answer as further evidence of our paranoia, I foresee us being called once again to the role of "A Prophetic Minority." The call is as old as the Old Testament prophets when Israel was in exile and as new as the remnant of believers in anti-Christian countries who are true to the faith even under the threat of persecution and death. It will be twice as hard for American Evangelicals to accept this call because we have been blessed to live in a nation where God is trusted and Biblical truth has been respected by a majority of our people. The transition will be traumatic, but not by surprise. Out of the stories of exile in the Old Testament and dispersion in the New Testament, the model for a prophetic minority is already set.

****

SEEING ALL THINGS WHOLE
A PROPHETIC MINORITY

Dare we take the Biblical option for the revitalization of the Evangelical initiative? Dare we answer the call for us to be once again "A Prophetic Minority"? James Davison Hunter, in his book *To Change the World*, gives us the vision that we need. Through misunderstanding, prejudice, and tribalism, we are called to be "The Faithful Presence."[4]

---

4. Hunter, *To Change the World*, 280.

PILGRIMS ON A JOURNEY

First, we will have to change our thinking from being residents-in-place to becoming pilgrims on a journey. Once a day, my wife and I change worlds. Shortly after noon, we leave our comfortable condo and our retired neighbors for a walk through Marina Park in downtown Kirkland, Washington. After walking through the intersection at the center of town identified as "Pride Center" in tribute to the LBGTQ community, we enter Marina Park. One step into the park turns us into a minority. Middle Eastern, Asian, and Indian families dominate the seashore. German-speaking couples walk by. Muslim women carry their babies in their arms. Turbaned Sri Lankan men strike a posture of dignity. Mixed in are parents of African and Hispanic ancestry pushing their wide-eyed babies into an uncertain world. I invite you to join us as I share our experiences in my book *Confessions of a Streetwalker.*

Whether we like it or not, this is America of the future. White supremacists, religious bigots, and social isolationists are going to fail in their efforts to retain tribal purity and privilege. Advocates for equality will take their place with the same claims for purity and privilege. In between the extremes, there will be the call for tolerance. With it will come the expectation that Christian evangelism is a violation of the prevailing mode of tolerance and equality. Evidence is already coming in that Christians find it hard to evangelize neighbors whom they get to know personally. How can God send such good people to hell? Practical universalism is a threat to the integrity of the Gospel message.

Most of us have to confess that we are cozy and complacent residents-in-place, enjoying the comforts of an affluent age. Are we ready to live out the message of the song, "This world is not my home; I'm just a-passing through"? To think of ourselves as pilgrims on a journey when we enjoy all of the comforts of residents-in-place is a paradigm shift of highest magnitude.

PROPHETS IN A BULLY PULPIT

Second, we will have to accept prophets who speak uncomfortable truth to the community of faith as well as to the surrounding culture. Teddy Roosevelt is known for the "bully pulpit" from which he, as president of the United States, could speak uncomfortable truth to the issues of day. The same is true for all prophets, religious or secular.

Jesus is our example. Whenever He spoke to needy persons outside the faith, such as the Samaritan woman at the well, He led with grace and followed with truth. But, when He addressed religious insiders, such as Pharisees in the Temple, He led with truth and followed with grace. No role is more difficult than to be a "Truth-Teller," especially when addressing the Church itself. Our preference is to lead as a "Grace-giver," sensing the needs of our people and responding with therapeutic palliatives. Old Testament prophets of Israel's exile, from Isaiah to Micah, are hardly the role models of leadership to which we aspire today. Yet, as I weigh the challenges we face, I find special affinity with the prophet Nehemiah. In fact, I wrote a book under the title *Becoming Nehemiah: Leading with Significance. In* Nehemiah's ministry I see this truth: "The journey of leadership is the story of moving from one crucible to another as the individual moves higher in visibility and greater in responsibility."[5] For those who speak the truth, a crucible awaits.

Are we ready to hear our brothers and sisters reject us as Isaiah was rejected by his people? Are we ready to walk fully exposed through the streets for three years as a warning to those who will not hear the truth? Prophets who speak the truth open themselves to the stigma of being castigated as bigots, paranoids, and fear-mongers. Furthermore, to be a prophet is to give up our thirst for instant success and be faithful to the truth even though we may never see our faith become sight. After Isaiah answered the call of God and received the hot coal of truth on his lips, he accepted his assignment to call Israel to repentance. But, when told

5. McKenna, *Becoming Nehemiah*, 30.

that he would be received by deaf ears, blind eyes, and hard hearts, he dared to ask, *"For how long, O Lord?"* (Is. 6:11). He didn't like the answer, and neither will we. God said, *"Until the Lord has sent everyone away and the land is utterly forsaken"* (Is. 6:12) and only stumps are left. But, in a future time that Isaiah will never see, out of those stumps will come the *"holy seed"* (Is.6:13) for the redemption of Israel. Are we, impatient disciples of the Radical Now, ready for the timing of the prophetic task?

CITIZENS PLANTING GARDENS

Third, even as pilgrims on a journey in a strange country, we are still called to be citizens planting gardens. Both Paul and Peter take a firm stand for Christians obeying public authorities who are ordained of God to protect the health, welfare and safety of its citizens. Civil disobedience is not an option for Christians unless public authorities try to take away our religious freedom or take over the ordained authority of the Church for human redemption. In the climate of religious freedom that democracy gives us, Christians cannot be isolates. Our witness must include personal engagement with the human needs and social conflicts of our secular, as well as our religious, world.

What does it mean to be a Christian planting gardens in a secular society? As a college, university, and seminary president I felt called to live out John Wesley's profound truth, *"The gospel of Christ knows of no religion but social; no holiness but social holiness.* My calling to social holiness came in the opportunity to serve in city, state, national, and even international affairs as a Christian leader. Civic as well as educational and religious affairs became the setting for my "bully pulpit." While at Spring Arbor College, I served as president of the Rotary Club in Jackson, Michigan; at Seattle Pacific University I led the educational sector for United Way of Seattle; and at Asbury Theological Seminary I did the study for Bluegrass Tomorrow, a look at the future of social services in the greater Lexington area. I cite these ventures not to brag, but to illustrate the potential for Christians who care about their community and their world. Democracy that is determined by the will of the people and enacted within the guardrails of human liberty meets the biblical standard for Christian obedience to public authority. Liberal democracy, with such social programs as Social Security and Medicare, still qualify under the aegis of health and welfare even though they were originally opposed as leaning toward government control. Martin Marty has noted that we are living in a time when "The people who are good at being civil often lack strong convictions and people who have strong convictions often lack civility."[6]

Our call, as Christians, is to be persons who embody what Marty calls "convicted civility." His view confirms my position that a Christian is a person who will make both sides mad. Tribalism is a stereotype that makes puppets of persons who hold no convictions above and beyond the emotions of the moment. Are we, as Christian citizens, living in a time of exile ready to be exemplars for convicted civility? The fertile soil of social holiness awaits us.

SERVANTS SACRIFICING SELF

Fourth, as a prophetic minority we are called to be servants who sacrifice themselves for the needs of others. Wait just a moment. Our immediate assumption is that we are to give to the lost, the least, and the littlest among us, wherever and whoever they may be. Matthew 25, the picture of the final judgment, confirms the fact that if the Spirit of Christ is within us, we will give ourselves to the hungry, the homeless, the widowed and the imprisoned. But, where does the obligation begin? The answer of Scripture may surprise us. In the earliest Christian church established after Pentecost, the first obligation of servanthood was to care for the needy in the newly established Body of Christ. Our capitalist mindset may rebel against the thought that our Spirit-filled ancestors held *"all things in common"* (Acts 2:44) so that everyone's needs were met. Is this an aberration on the assumption that each of us is responsible for

6. Quoted in Mouw, *Uncommon Decency,* 14.

our own welfare and will find the resources to meet our needs? The answer is "No." Despite all of the benefits of an affluent society and the hopes of a trickle-down system of economic success, there are those in the community of faith who have desperate needs. Whether we agree or not, the first obligation of the Body of Christ is to care for the needs of those among us who have fallen through the safety net of the system. Paul gives us the standard for our servanthood. As he travelled far and wide among the newly established churches of Gentile Christians in Asia Minor and Greece, he called them to their responsibility for Jewish Christians in Jerusalem who were suffering in abject poverty for their faith. Paul went so far as to test their faith by the offering they collected for the needs of brothers and sisters who were so distant and so different. Peter, in his second Epistle, reinforced Paul's commands by charging believers in exile with the responsibility for serving their brothers and sisters in need (I Peter 4:7).

At the same time, we cannot dismiss the need for Christians to reach out to the hurts of the lost, least, and littlest beyond us as well as among us. "Risk-taking" must be added to our servanthood and our sacrifice. This is the Spirit of Jesus Christ that we cannot deny. The lesson came to me in the most radical of ways. While President at Seattle Pacific College, I received a surprise call from Governor Dan Evans. He asked me to chair his Select Commission for the Study of Gambling in the State of Washington. As a non-gambler I was shocked, but the governor said that they needed a chairman who would bring integrity as well as independence to the conflicted field of bingo, card games, slot machines, and lotteries. After prayer and consultation, I accepted the position. The next day the Seattle Post-Intelligencer made the announcement that the governor had a appointed a chairman for his gambling commission who was better known for "guarding the holy font." Later, there were threats of a burning cross on the lawn of the president's home at Seattle Pacific as well as newspaper columns questioning the power of the Commission against the widespread gambling interests. To make a long story short, we were able to draw up guidelines against corruption for bingo, card games, and slots and put brakes on the powerful forces seeking a state lottery. The win was only temporary. It was just a matter time before the advocates for a state lottery won out.

Was my leadership futile? I think that I know how Isaiah felt when he cried out, *"For how long, O Lord?" (Isaiah 6:11)* when he saw no results for his ministry. Whatever the case, God taught me the truth that we are called to leadership that is servanthood with sacrifice and risk-taking. A plaque on the wall of my office recognizing my contribution to the quality of life in our Seattle community is a reminder that God gave me a chance to show how a Christian serves in a secular society with integrity and character. I would do it again.

SEERS OF HOPE

Fifth, and finally, in a prophetic minority we are to be "futurists." It is time to embrace and enact the monumental truth of Jesus' promise for the coming of the Holy Spirit, *"He will show you things to come."* (John 16:13). Once we accept this gift, our time perspective shifts from the Radical "Now" to the biblical "Then." This does not mean that we fall into the fixation of an Apocalyptic mindset or adopt the lockstep of a Dispensational theology. Futurists in a prophetic minority share Peter's two-sided declaration of the Day of the Lord. On the bottom side is the dire prediction, *"But the day of the Lord will come like a thief. The heavens will disappear with a roar, the elements will be destroyed by fire, and the earth and everything in it will be laid bare."* (II Peter 3:10). Fear might paralyze the hearers of Peter's prediction. But no, he uses it to ask the question, *"What kind of people ought you to be? You ought to live holy and godly lives as you look forward to the day of the Lord and speed its coming."* (II Peter 3:11–12).

On the top side of the prediction is the hope-filled promise, *"But in keeping with his promise, we are looking forward to a new heaven and a new earth, the home of righteousness."* (II Peter 3:13). All esoteric interpretations of the prediction and the promise disappear in Peter's practical application, *"So then, dear friends, since you are looking forward to this, make every effort to be found spot-less, blameless and at peace with him.*" (II Peter 3:14).

Over the years, I have tried to speak prophetically as a Chris-tian about the future. In a quick scan of the shelf that holds my books, I see:

The Coming Great Awakening, a volume in which I trace the stirrings of the Spirit for spiritual revival among college students;

The Leader's Legacy, a call for Christian leaders to "build on the past, give momentum to the present, and assure greater things for the future";

Megatruth, in which I project Jesus' promise, "He will show you things to come" into the realities of a future where the Spirit of God balances our short-term view with long-term vision and counters our pessimism with the optimism of His promise; and

The Posterity Gospel with the conclusion that we need to "Let go of the past, lean into the future, and follow The Christ."

While I do not claim a prophetic vision for the future, I do claim the stutter steps that have led me to the personal hope for eternal life and the social hope for a great awakening in our con-flicted age.

Walt Disney died before Disney World in Florida was fin-ished. At the time of its grand opening, Walter Cronkite was the master of ceremonies. As he sat on the dais with Mrs. Walt Disney, he looked out over the Fantasy World and turned to his hostess to say, "I know that you wish that Mr. Disney was here to see this sight." Mrs. Disney answered, "If Mr. Disney hadn't seen it first, we wouldn't be seeing it today."

Futurists of the prophetic minority see first what God has promised for His beleaguered Church and our conflicted world. As dire as the daily news may be, the Good News of the Gos-pel cannot be canceled and the vision of His Coming cannot be dimmed. Our job description as futurists for the cause of Christ is already written. We are called to be pilgrims on a journey, proph-ets with a bully pulpit, citizens planting gardens, servants sacrific-ing self, and, most of all, seers of hope who see first what God has promised. This is our legacy of holiness and wholeness for the current and coming generation. It is a debt we owe; it is our calling to fulfill.

11

Seeing All Things Whole
Reprise

GOD'S GRAND DESIGN

"Reprise" is the musical term for repeating the verse of a song, perhaps with new timing, modulations, and accents. For me, reprise
for my story is just that. In the final words of this book, I want to
sing another verse of *Seeing All Things Whole; My Calling to Fulfill*
with the surprise of new meaning for the way we see all things
whole.

SEEING SMALL

It is time for the rarest of confessions. As a retired university and
seminary president, I confess that it is hard *not* be "Number 1."
How well I remember the pride of being greeted as "Mr. President." How well I remember the times when I spoke and someone
listened. How vividly I still see the book, articles and pictures that
carry my name. To say that I am spoiled is an understatement.

Being featured as a star on center stage is long gone. Oh, how I miss those moments!

I recall a conversation with Governor Dan Evans of Washington after he resigned from the Senate and took the presidency of Evergreen State University. In quiet confidence, he said, "Dave, after you have been Number One, it is hard to start over." He was referring to the fact that, as our esteemed governor, he was Number One in our State. But when he completed his terms and won a seat in the U.S. Senate, he had to start all over again as a junior senator in a rigid seniority system. The presidency of Evergreen State University put him back at Number One.

As a person who served 33 consecutive years as president of three institutions of Christian higher education, I also confess that it is hard to no longer be Number One. Retirement is a testing time for the presidential ego. Even with the revered title of President Emeritus, reminders of my lowered position come daily. Around our condo, no one knows me as Dr. McKenna. Even former students send Facebook messages addressed to "Dave." I have no secretary to write my letters, no custodian to clean my office, and no parking place with the self-glorifying words, "RESERVED FOR THE PRESIDENT." When journals and newsletters come from the institutions where I served, I confess that my first run through the pages is to see if my name is mentioned. Even in the institutional histories that have been written, I critically scan the context. More often than not, I feel slighted and growl, "Those historians don't know the whole story."

Two visits to the Seattle Pacific University campus sum up my confession. In the 1980's our oldest son, Douglas, was a professor in the School of Business. Proudly, I walked up to the entrance and stopped to read again the plaque identifying the School as "McKenna Hall." When I walked inside, I was greeted by a bright student receptionist who asked, "May I help you?" "Yes," I answered. "I am David McKenna looking for the office of my son, Dr. Douglas McKenna." "Sure," she responded as she began to scour the list of faculty offices. When her finger reached the end of list without results, she looked up with the innocence of a new-born baby and asked, "How do you spell that name?"

Twenty years later, I tried again. Rob, our youngest son, is now a professor at Seattle Pacific University in the School of Industrial and Organizational Psychology. His office is in Watson Hall, but they have no receptionist on duty. While standing in the lobby trying to find my way to Rob's office, a professorial-looking man walked in. I hurried to catch him and ask, "Can you point me to Dr. Rob McKenna's office?" "Sure," he answered, and then posed the query, "You must be Dr. McKenna's father." Inwardly, I was screaming, "It's Dr. David McKenna, you lummox."

Writing your own autobiography is even tougher on the ego. John Gardner tells the story of a lonely, little girl peering through the curtains at a group of youngsters playing on the lawn. A solicitous adult saw her plight and chirped, "Look, they're coming inside now so that you can play with them." The little girl looked back at him and asked wistfully, "But what if they don't care?"[1] An autobiography is a bit like that. Even if you purposely avoid an exaggerated show of ego, the story is still a form of self-adulation. So, I wonder, when this book is published and available to the public, what will be the response? My fear is the same as the response of the little girl at the window. What if they don't care? I will have to take that chance.

SEEING BIG

Now that I have exposed the immaturity of my self-concept at the age of 95, let me tell you how the Holy Spirit helped me grow up. Jan and I were having morning devotions and reading Paul's account of the jealousies that were shredding the unity and draining the energy of the Corinthian Church. One faction favors the leadership of Paul; the other faction rallies around Apollos. The result is an inevitable clash of monumental egos. Paul has all of the credentials for claiming intellectual and spiritual superiority,

---

1. Gardner, *Self-Renewal*, 8.

but Apollos is the favorite son of a populist movement within the Church. Will Paul exercise his apostolic authority to quash the rebellion? He chose that option when evil men were threatening to break apart the Philippian Church over the question of circumcision. Claiming superior authority, his credentials destroy the opposition:

> *If anyone else thinks that he has reasons to put confidence in the flesh, I have more: circumcised on the eighth day, of the people of Israel, of the tribe of Benjamin, a Hebrew of Hebrews, in regard to the law a Pharisee, as for zeal, persecuting the church, as for legalistic righteousness, faultless. (Phil.3:4–6)*

In Corinth, however, he takes the opposite view because he is dealing with Apollos, a brother in Christ. So, rather than exercising his apostolic authority, he calms the waters and resolves the conflict with the humblest of words,

> *"I planted the seed, Apollos watered it, but God made it grow." (I Corinthians 3:6)*

This perspective on leadership profoundly changed me. For the sake of the Gospel, Paul steps aside from an ego-driven demand for recognition as a leader in order to become a role player in God's grand drama of redemption. The result is what I call "God's Grand Design" in which the whole is greater than the sum of its parts. Leaders who go solo may gain their honors, but they will never know the highest honor of all—to have the Holy Spirit seal our leadership with the beauty of wholeness that is far greater than the sum of its parts. Once I had this insight, I was set free from ego-driven leadership. The fact cannot be denied. There is more meaning in being a role player in God's redemptive drama under the inspiration of His Spirit than pretending to be the indispensable star in just a slice of the story. Let me tell you what I learned.

SEEING ANEW

In Christian leadership, we need to see the whole picture. Someplace back in the 1970's we had to decide how to respond to the rising tide of concern about social justice, especially for the Black community. As a trustee of the Bread for the World board, I became a friend of John Perkins, a fellow member. Our spirits blended and I invited John to speak in chapel at Seattle Pacific University. Of course, he won the hearts of all who listened. Humility plus compassion plus vision came together in his address. After we left the Bread for the World board, years went by without connection with John. Then, during President Philip Eaton's administration, John was brought into close association with Seattle Pacific through its initiative for reconciliation. What started out as a seed of thought had now matured into the John Perkins Center for Reconciliation. When John came back again to personalize the inauguration for the Center, I understand that he asked someone, "What ever happened to that kid president who was here many years ago?" Do you see the beauty of systemic holiness in this story? What greater joy can we have than to be a role player in the great redemptive drama.

In Christian leadership, we need to say "We." One of my favorite sermon illustrations is the story of the organist who won all of Europe in its concert halls. His musical gift was matched only by the size of his ego. He was a prima donna at its extreme. Behind the scene of all his concerts, however, was an assistant who pumped the bellows for the instrument. In one of the performances in the grandest of concert halls, the artist rose to his egotistical peak. Striding into the concert hall he took bow after bow before being seated at the organ. His hands rose with one last flourish before dropping down on the keys for the first majestic chord. But when his fingers hit the keys, nothing happened. In panic, the organ master raised his hands again, waved another flourish, and dropped them down again. Only silence. Vivid with rage, the master raced behind the curtains where the lad was pumping the bellows. He stormed, "Who do you think you are? You have ruined my concert and the greatest moment of my life." With just a wry smile, the boy of the bellows simply said, "Say, "We' Mister."

In Christian leadership we need to change from being stars of our own story to role-players in God's grand redemptive drama. Sheer delight takes over when we are asked about the exploits of our leadership. Self becomes the focus to which all aspects of our life and leadership are drawn. Our story may be good and true to ourselves, but it must be told in the context of the larger scene of Christ's atonement and God's will. How small our self-story is in comparison with God's story. How fractured our self-story is in comparison with the wholeness of the Holy Spirit at work in us. How weak we are when we fail to gain strength from working together with our peers in the faith.

SEEING WHOLE

The minute that I write these words, my mind goes back to one of the most significant moments in my presidential career. While at Asbury we received a gift from the Beeson family or nearly sixty-six million dollars. I would like to take credit for it, but I can't. The name of Dr. J.C. McPheeters, second president of Asbury, comes up frequently. He hunted and fished with Ralph Beeson, ate Orlean Beeson's dinners, slept in their home, and prayed with them. Yet, believe it or not, he never asked them for money. Instead, he told them the latest stories of God at work in the lives of faculty and students at Asbury. Time and time again, Ralph and Orlean sent him home with significant gifts to address the needs revealed in his stories.

Where do I fit in? The Beeson estate gift was received during my administration and I get the credit for it. In fact, when we had a press conference to announce the gift, I was asked how my leadership made the gift possible. Paul's paradigm for the Corinthian Church calls me to a halt. The fact is that Dr. McPheeters planted the seed, I watered it, and God made it grow. The shift does not bother me. In fact, I find new freedom in the role as a waterer of the seeds that someone else has planted. Even more important is the truth that God alone made the endowment grow.

Out of this experience, in my mind's eye I see what I call "God's Grand Design" in which the whole is far greater than the sum of its parts and the beauty exceeds human imagination. It is now the guide for my life and leadership. Here it is:

> Paul is the planter, Apollos is the waterer, and God is the grower.

Reflecting on this paradigm, my thoughts go back to seeing my life as a spiritual odyssey. I applied the parts of the paradigm to each of the chapters in this book that describe my role as a college, university, and seminary president. History blew wide open for me. Sometimes a planter, sometimes a waterer, I now sense rich connections with those who proceeded me, those who worked with me, and those who followed me. Voila! I also have a new glimpse of the redemptive drama in our age – past, present and future. Best of all, I see how God, and God alone, gives the growth when we serve as planters or waterers.

A TAPESTRY OF GRACE

At the age of 95, I am face-to-face with the critical question, "How do I want to be remembered?" All of my degrees and achievements fall away and I realize that my highest honor is to be remembered as a servant/leader who is faithful to those who follow. Even now I see the words on a recent email from a person who excels as an executive leader in a Christian university:

> I am so very grateful for you, without whom I would not have the opportunity to make *any* contribution to Christian higher education.

Put all other kudos aside. My highest honor is to receive an unexpected word of thanks from those who come after me. You will understand why I am singing this prayer as I write:

O may all who come behind us Find us faithful,
May the fire of our devotion Light their way.
May the footprints that we leave, Lead them to believe,
And the lives we live Inspire them to obey.
O may all who come behind us Find us faithful.[2]

This then is my legacy of a lifetime. Weaving the threads of grace together, I glimpse the whole cloth and the grand design in the tapestry of God's good and perfect will for my life.

**I want holiness, the indwelling Spirit, as my experience with wholeness, personal and social, as its evidence;

**I want to be known as a role player in God's great redemptive drama, planting and watering seeds, with the growth exclusively given by God. And, finally,

**I want to be found faithful to all who come behind me.

No small order for the Tabernacle Kid who still struggles with the demands of perfection and the temptations of self-interest. For those struggles, I can only appeal to Oswald Chambers' benediction, *"Leave the broken, irreversible past in His hands and step out into the invincible future with Him."*[3] It is in the tapestry of grace that I find my invincible future. If others see the fire of my devotion lighting their way; if others see my footprints leading them to believe; and if others see the life I have lived as an inspiration to obey, I ask nothing more. Before Him I bow and to Him I give all the glory. Amen and Amen.

---

2. Lyrics by Jon Mohr
3. Chambers, *My Utmost*, entry for December 31.

Biographical Brief 2024

DAVID MCKENNA HAS SERVED more than 60 years in American higher education with faculty appointments at The Ohio State University and the University of Michigan in preparation for the call to 33 consecutive years as a president in Christian higher education. Beginning in 1961 at Spring Arbor College (now University), McKenna advanced a junior college into a four-year Christian liberal arts college; at Seattle Pacific University, he led the transition from a four-year college to university status; and at Asbury Theological Seminary he guided the process to receive the largest single grant ever given to a free-standing graduate school of theology. He retired as president emeritus of each institution, leaving his career in higher education to write, speak, and consult on subjects related to leadership in higher education and ministry. In 2003, he retired as chair emeritus of the Board of Trustees at Spring Arbor University.

McKenna holds the Bachelor of Arts degree in History from Western Michigan University, Master of Divinity from Asbury Theological Seminary, and the Master of Arts in Counseling Psychology and the Doctor of Philosophy in Higher Education from the University of Michigan. He has been awarded ten honorary doctorates, named a Paul Harris Fellow by Rotary International, honored by Stanley and Dorothy Kresge's endowment for the David L. McKenna Christian Leaders Scholarship for business students at Seattle Pacific University, and recognized as First Citizen of Seattle by The Municipal League in 1976.

Additional honors have come from Spring Arbor University with the David and Janet McKenna Carillon Tower, Seattle Pacific University with the David McKenna Hall for the School of Business, Government and Economics, Asbury Theological Seminary with the David and Janet McKenna Chapel, and Immanuel University (Hyderabad, India) with the McKenna Center for Leadership.

As a leader in American higher education, McKenna served as founding chair for the Christian College Consortium (parent organization for the Council of Christian College & Universities) and secretary for the National Association of Independent Colleges and Universities. In 1980, he was a finalist for the position of Secretary of Education in President Ronald Reagan's Cabinet.

As a religious leader ordained in the Free Methodist Church, McKenna has held the position of vice-president in the National Association of Evangelicals and in the North American section of the World Methodist Council. While serving as a consulting editor for the magazine *Christianity Today*, he also became known as a national radio commentator with the weekly sign-off, "You have heard the thoughts and felt the heartbeat of David McKenna." Forty-six books, ranging across the fields of psychology, biblical commentary, Christian leadership, history, and theology add to his legacy of leadership.

David and Janet McKenna celebrate their 74th wedding anniversary in 2024. They are parents of four children, Douglas, Debra, Suzanne, and Robert, twelve grandchildren, and nine great-grandchildren. A lakeside condo in Kirkland, Washington is their retirement home.

Books Published by David L. McKenna

The Urban Crisis (1968) Zondervan

Awake, My Conscience (1977) Light and Life Press Winona Lake, IN

Contemporary Issues for Evangelical Christians (1977) Reprint by Baker *The Jesus Model* (1977, Second Printing 1979) Word

The Psychology of Jesus: The Dynamics of Christian Wholeness (1977) Reprint by Word

The Communicator's Commentary: Mark (1982) Word

MegaTruth: The Church in the Age of Information (1986) Here's Life Publishers

Power to Follow; Grace to Lead (1986) Word

The Communicator's Commentary: Job (1986) Word

Renewing Our Ministry (1986) Word

The Whisper of His Grace (1987) Word

Discovering Job (1989) Guideposts

Love Your Work (1989) Shaw

The Coming Great Awakening (1990) IVP

The Works of David L. McKenna: (1993) ATS

When Our Parents Need Us Most (1994) Shaw

BOOKS PUBLISHED BY DAVID L. McKENNA

The Communicator's Commentary: Isaiah 1-39 (1994) Word

The Communicator's Commentary: Isaiah 40-66 (1994) Word

A Future with a History: The Wesleyan Witness of the Free Methodist Church (1997) Light and Life Press

Growing Up in Christ (1998) Light and Life Press

Journey through a Bypass: The Story of an Open Heart (1998) Life and Life Press

What a Time to be a Wesleyan: Anticipating the 21st Century (1999) Beacon Hill

The Christian Family Library: A Collection of 36 Books for a Three-year Reading Program, General Editor. (2001) Family Christian Press

How to Read a Christian Book (2001) Baker

Wesleyan Leadership in Troubled Times: Confronting the Culture; Challenging the Church (2003) Beacon Hill

The Preacher's Commentary Commentaries on Mark, Job, and Isaiah I and II (2003) Thomas Nelson

Never Blink in a Hailstorm and Other Lessons of Leadership (2005) Baker.

Never Steal a Paperclip (2008) OMS Literature

Becoming Nehemiah (2005) Beacon Hill

Leading with Significance: (Published in South Africa, United Kingdom, New Zealand and Australia

A Leader's Legacy: The Gift of Greater Things (2006) Barclay Press

Retirement Is Not for Sissies (2008) Barclay Press

A Stroke of Grace: Hope for Those Who Suffer and Those Who Care (2008) Xulon (Co-authored with Patricia McKenna Seraydarian, sister)

Stewards of a Sacred Trust: CEO Selection, Transition and Development for Boards of Christ-centered Organizations (2010) ECFA

When God Laughs with Us: The Lighter Side of Leadership (2010) WipfandStock

Christ-centered Higher Education: Memory, Meaning and Momentum for the 21st Century (2012) Cascade Books

Christ-centered Leadership: The Incarnational Difference (2013) Cascade Books

The Succession Principle: How Leaders Make Leaders (2015) Cascade Books

Confessions of a Street Walker: Molly, Me, and Jan Make Three (2016) Wipf and Stock

Call of the Chair: Leading the Board of the Christ-centered Organization. ECFA (2017)

The Posterity Gospel: Managing Our Spiritual Wealth. Light and Life Press (2018)

The Unfinished Gospel: Failure Is Not Final. Light and Life Press (2019)

The Triumphs of His Grace: A Spiritual Odyssey. Wipf and Stock (2022)

Seeing All Things Whole: My Calling to Fulfill. Wipf and Stock (2024)

Donald E. Demaray is the author of David L. McKenna's biography, *With His Joy: The Life and Leadership of David McKenna*, Light and Life Press, 2000.

Bibliography

2019 Book of Discipline of the Free Methodist Church. Indianapolis: Light + Life, 2109.

A Concept to Keep. Spring Arbor University Press, 2003.

Bellah, Robert. *Habits of the Heart.* New York: Harper and Row, 1986.

Bevins, Winfield H. "Pneumatology in John Wesley's Theological Method," *The Asbury Journal,* Vol.58, No. 2, 101-114.

Chambers, Oswald. *My Utmost for His Highest.* Oswald Chambers Publications, 1935.

Gardner, John W. *Self-Renewal: The Individual and the Innovative Society.* New York: W. W. Norton, 1981.

Grubb, Norman Percy. *Modern Viking: The Story of Abraham Vereide, Pioneer in Christian Leadership.* Tauranga, New Zealand: Papamoa, 2018.

Hatch, Nathan. *The Democratization of American Christianity.* New Haven, CT: Yale University Press, 1989.

Henry, Carl F. H. *The Uneasy Conscience of Modern Fundamentalism.* Grand Rapids: William B. Eerdmans, 1947.

Holmes, Arthur F. *The Idea of a Christian College.* Grand Rapids: William B. Eerdmans, 1975.

Horney, Karen, *Neurosis and Human Growth: The Struggle for Self-Realization.* Oxon, UK: Routledge.

Hunter, James Davison. *To Change the World: The Irony, Tragedy, and Possibility of Christianity in the Late Modern World.* Oxford University Press, 2010.

Keeping the Concept. Spring Arbor University Press, 2004.

McKenna, David L. *A Future with a History.* Winona Lake, IN: Light and Life, 1969.

———. *Becoming Nehemiah: Leading With Significance.* Kansas City: Beacon Hill, 2005.

———, ed. *The Urban Crisis.* Grand Rapids: Zondervan, 1969.

Mouw, Richard H. *Uncommon Decency: Christian Civility in an Uncivil World.* Downers Grove, IL: IVP Books, 2010.

Schaeffer, Francis, and C. Everett Koop. *Whatever Happened to the Human Race?* Wheaton, IL: Crossway, 1979.

BIBLIOGRAPHY

Tertullian. *The Prescription Against Heretics.* Beloved, 2014.

Trueblood, Elton. *A New Man for Our Time.* New York: Harper & Row, 1970.

Watson, C. Hoyt. *The Amazing Story of Sargeant Jacob DeShazer.* Winona Lake, IN: Light and Life, 1963.

Wesley, Charles, "A Prayer for Children," *The Poetical Works of John and Charles Wesley*, Vol. 6.

Wesley, John. *Journal*, June 11, 1739.

Wesley, John and Charles Wesley. *Hymns and Sacred Poems.* 1739.